50 Ways to Improve Your Business English

(without too much effort!)

by Ken Taylor

Lulu Publishing
www.lulu.com

ISBN 978-0-244-67896-8

Author acknowledgements
A special thank you to my wife Christine and my old friend Rupert Matthews for reading all the drafts and for their comments and feedback, most of which I have acted upon.
Thanks also to Ian McMaster, the Editor-in-Chief of Business Spotlight magazine for his help and encouragement.

Ken Taylor
ktaylor868@aol.com

Foreword

Do you sometimes feel insecure when speaking English in a business setting? Does your mind sometimes go blank as the English words disappear from your memory during an international phone call?
Do you sometimes feel irritated when you can't express exactly what you really want to say during the meeting?
If the answer to any of those questions is "Yes!" – then this is the book for you.

This is a self-help manual for those business people:
- who have English as their second language
- who need English in their work
- who have little time to improve their linguistic competence.

You can use this book in several ways:
- You can read it from cover to cover on the aeroplane or on holiday.
- You can "dip-read" or "skim-read" and pick out the bits that look interesting for you.
- You can do the self-assessment on page 10 and follow the advice given when you check the results.
- You can look at the index and choose those chapters that deal with the problem areas you know you have.
- You can give this book as a present to someone you know will benefit from it (and borrow it back if you need to!).

Learning takes time. But there are some short cuts. The 50 tips in this book will allow you to make noticeable improvements with the minimum of effort. So whichever way you choose to use this book – get started now! Read the introduction or read the summary at the end. Read the Presentations Module if you make presentations in English or assess your grammar in the Grammar Module. Do something, anything, to break into the book. And remember that doing five minutes every day is better than planning hour-long homework sessions that never take place because something urgent comes up that you have to do instead.
If you have read this foreword without too much difficulty you are at the right language level to benefit from this book.

Index

Introduction

"If at first you don't succeed, try, try again. Then quit. No use being a damn fool about it."

W C Fields

What kind of English should you speak?

English is not the most widely spoken language in the world if you only count native speakers. It's the second after Chinese. But if we were to add on second language speakers then English becomes number one. It's roughly estimated that about two billion people can communicate in English – of whom about 400 million are native speakers. So we should keep in mind that speakers of English as a second language outnumber native speakers by over three to one.

In school your teachers used either British English or American English as a model. You were taught to try to become perfect speakers of "Oxford" English or of "Harvard" English. And this has coloured your way of looking at the language ever since. Everyone tried to get ten out of ten in school language tests – perfection was demanded and grades depended on it. But in real life language is an imperfect tool. And any attempt to become a "perfect" speaker of English is doomed to failure.

Native speakers are not necessarily the best models for you.

Firstly their language is often filled with idiomatic and slang expressions, which second language speakers do not always understand – "Do you fancy a nosh after the do with a drop of the other?"[1] Or their language is culture bound – "I was on a really sticky wicket and was totally stumped."[2] In this case the speaker is using language from the game of cricket to describe an everyday situation. In the States you might hear an American use baseball terms in business – "I really struck out on that deal."[3]

Secondly native speakers often speak very quickly and with strong regional dialects. This makes it difficult even for other native speakers to grasp their meaning. And they find it impossible to modify this accent and speed to suit the international arena.

Thirdly native speakers may use over complicated grammatical constructions

---

[1] Would you like a meal and a drink after the event?

[2] I was in a difficult situation and had no solution to the problem.

[3] I failed to get a deal.

and a very wide vocabulary. Their language is then extremely difficult for the one and a half billion second language speakers. It has been estimated that an educated native speaker may be able to use eight thousand words in their active vocabulary. A good second language speaker may have only three to three and a half thousand words at their disposal.

So, if you do not use native speakers as your model for working internationally, what should you do?

Aim to become an excellent speaker of International English.

- Communicate in Standard English so that you are understood both by Mr Smith and Mr Yamamoto. You don't need idiomatic and slang expressions to impress your international business partners – quite the reverse in fact.
- Don't worry about your accent. It may be noticeable. That's fine as long as it does not interfere with understanding. It is part of your charm and cultural background.
- Speak at the speed you want to be spoken to. In other words, model good international English especially to your native speaker colleagues. It helps them modify their language and makes it easier for you to deal with them.
- Aim to build up an active vocabulary of about four thousand words. This will be enough to enable you to negotiate well, make good presentations, run effective meetings, write good emails etc. – in other words carry out all those tasks expected of you in your business field.
- KISS your communication – Keep It Short and Simple. Use short words, short sentences and short paragraphs. It's easier for your business partners to understand (and it's easier for you to produce!).

When you use good International English, your business partners, both native and second language speakers, will perceive you as an effective communicator. And many second language speakers will prefer to do business with you rather than with a hard-to-understand native speaker.

How do you learn?

Do you remember the lessons and teachers you liked most at school? If you do this might help you in the process of identifying your particular learning style. We are all different and we all learn in different ways.

For example, when you were studying English at school and your teacher gave you ten new words to learn, how did you go about it? Did you have a photographic memory that enabled you to look at the list once and then remember everything? Probably not as most of us have to work hard at fixing things in our memories. Perhaps you sat and read and re-read the words – occasionally covering up the English and trying to remember from the translation. Or did you draw doodles and pictures to help stimulate your memory? Or perhaps you stood up and walked around with the paper in your hand, saying the words aloud to yourself? Or perhaps you did all of these? The 50 ways to improve your business English include a mixture of learning activities that suit different learning styles. Try to get a feeling for the type of activity that works best for you. You can then concentrate on those exercises and approaches. So, make sure that what you plan to do is not only valuable as far as the content is concerned, but also that the method of learning is stimulating and motivating for you. Learning is more effective if it is fun and enjoyable.

What are the ten key improvement areas?
The choice of the ten areas covered by this book is based on long experience of working with international communication skills courses. Eight of the areas are the basic business communication skills we all need – the skills we also use in our business dealings in our first language. If we work in an international organisation, we need to write emails in English and make phone calls. We meet and negotiate with people. We make short presentations of ourselves, our organisations and our products or services.   It is simply a question of successfully transferring our business competence in our mother tongue to English (although this is easier said than done!). The two other areas are based on pure language competence - improving grammar and extending vocabulary. Most second language speakers mainly want to practice and improve their speaking skills. You feel that the more passive skills are a little easier to manage. With reading and writing you generally have more time to go back and check what you have done. With listening your passive vocabulary is larger than your active one, which gives you a more secure feeling.
A survey carried out by Business Spotlight in Germany asked its readers to list their biggest problems when working in English.   The eight business skill areas in this book cover the top eight business skills mentioned in the survey. They are put in descending order of difficulty according to the results of the survey. Two modules – Business Vocabulary and Grammar – were not included in the survey. They are placed at the end of the book.

What should your target be?

Imagine a scale of English language competence where 0 = absolute beginner and 5 = native speaker. Getting from level 0 to level 1 (survival English) will not take too long. But getting from level 4 (full professional competence) to level 5 might take a lifetime!

If you are at level 3 (competent intermediate) or 3+ you need to be realistic in your approach to language learning and improvement. You cannot expect a huge improvement across the board. Instead you need to make improvements in those areas where you gain the greatest benefit. This will also improve your self-confidence in specific situations and this, in turn, will gradually affect your general level of competence.

Do the self-assessment. This could help you decide where those areas of improvement should take place. But be realistic.

To parody a well-known phrase – "Improvements will be made immediately but miracles take a little longer!"

Self-assessment

"Experience is the worst teacher, it gives the test before the lesson."
Vernon Law (American baseball player)

To help you focus on your real needs take a few minutes to do the following self-assessment. This could save you time in the long run.
Assess the following statements on the 5-point scale.

A. Importance to me

	Very		Quite	.	Not
	5	4	3	2	1

1. I need to be able to socialize in English
2. I run or take part in meetings in English
3. I negotiate in English
4. I make telephone calls in English
5. I make presentations in English
6. I listen to people speaking with different accents in English
7. I need to read business texts in English
8. I write emails in English
9. I need to find the right word in English
10. I need my English grammar to be correct

B. My performance

	Poor	.	Fair	.	Excellent
	5	4	3	2	1

1. Socialising in English
2. Running or taking part in meetings in English
3. Negotiating in English
4. Making telephone calls in English
5. Presenting in English
6. Listening to people speaking with different accents in English
7. Reading business texts in English
8. Writing emails in English
9. Ability to find the right word in English
10. My use of English grammar

Just simply doing the assessment and thinking about your needs might well have crystallised your study priorities. But if you would like a more "mathematical" approach then add together the importance and performance scores for each of the ten skills. Any skill which scores 8 or over is of high priority. Any skill which scores 4 or under is of low priority.

If you still need help deciding on priorities between two or more skill areas with the same number of points then decide which of the skills you need most frequently.

This simple self-assessment allows you to select what you need from the rest of the book if you do not want to read it from cover to cover. Or you can start with the high priority chapters and go on to the others if and when you have the time.

Right! That was the easy part. Now it's up to you. If you want to improve your business English, you have to start somewhere. As the Nike advert says, "Just do it!"

Socialising and networking

"When all things are equal, people prefer to do business with friends. And they even prefer to do business with friends when things are not equal."

Mark McCormack

Most of us want to create long-term business relationships based on trust and mutual respect. This means that networking and socialising are important activities, especially when working internationally. In some cultures the relationship is even more important than the particular business in hand. Time and energy goes into building and maintaining good personal relationships in order to make difficult business discussions and decisions easier to handle. Here are five tips to improve the English you need to network and socialise in English.

1. Say hello properly

The first words you say set the scene for the rest of the relationship. "You never have a second chance to make a first impression" is an over-used saying that contains a great deal of truth. When we say "hello" we are telling our business partner how we are feeling about meeting him or her. And we have a large number of "hellos" to choose from. You can be highly formal – or very informal. Your partner is expected to mirror this feeling in their reply.

How would you reply to these greetings?

A. *It's an honour to meet you.*

B. *How do you do?*

C. *How are you?*

D. *How're things?*

E. *Hi there.*

F. *Wotcher!*

(You can find the answers below)[4]

But instead of simply reacting to other people, why not seize the initiative here and set the level of formality you prefer. Be proactive. This also means being flexible. If you don't want to sound too friendly because you want to bring up

---

[4] A. Thank you   B. How do you do?   C. Fine thanks. And you?   D. Great. And how're things with you?   E. Hi! F. Hi! ("Wotcher" is cockney slang and very informal.)

several complaints during the meeting, then choose a more formal greeting. If you've built up a good relationship over the phone or by email, then choose an informal greeting.

My favourite greeting when I meet someone for the first time is: *Nice to meet you.* It's friendly but business-like. It's easy to get the reply right as well – *Nice to meet you too.*

What do you say after you've said hello? Well, if this is a first meeting we often need to say who we are and this can cause cultural problems. In Germany for example business people might only offer their family names – *Schmidt.* Whilst in Sweden you might only be offered the first name – *Sven.* When working internationally use both names. This is useful information to match the business card you offer and it can allow you to be proactive again. Don't say, *"I'm Manfred Schmidt."* Then you are leaving your business partner to choose whether to call you *Manfred* or *Mr Schmidt.* Indicate what you want to be called – rather like James Bond in the movies. In the official MI6 meetings he introduces himself as *"Bond. James Bond."* In other words he's telling you to call him *Mr Bond.* His first name is simply for your information. But in the bar with the beautiful blonde he says, *"Hi there. I'm James, James Bond."* In other words he's telling her to call him by his first name. In most international business settings this last approach is probably the best one. Which means that your first two sentences would sound something like this, *"Nice to meet you. I'm Manfred, Manfred Schmidt."*

Remember:
- Be proactive.
- Choose the appropriate way of saying "hello".
- Be like James Bond.

Two Japanese businessmen are visiting a stand at a Hanover trade fair. They meet three German sales representatives, Heinz Schmidt, Franz Schmidt and Helmut Krantz. In correct German manner the first Mr Schmidt shakes hands with each of the Japanese and introduces himself with just his family name – "Schmidt. Schmidt." The two Japanese are then greeted by the second sales representative in the same way – "Schmidt. Schmidt. Slightly confused they move on to the third person and, taking the initiative, the first Japanese greets him – "Schmidt. Schmidt"!

2. Make active small talk

Some people love to small talk, others hate it. Some cultures demand it whilst others ignore it. In international business small talk can be extremely useful. By talking about neutral, non-controversial topics you can start to break the ice, get a feeling for the communication style of your partner and begin to tune your ear to their English. The neutral topics – the weather, the trip, the hotel, the town – are easy to talk about without disagreement. In Britain it is said that there are three taboo subjects for small talk – politics, sex and religion. Why? Because then it's easy to get into an argument. What you want to do instead is to build a platform of agreement on which to do the business. This platform of agreement helps when you might have to disagree later on in the meeting.

Even if you come from a country where small talk is not part of your culture, try to use it as an icebreaker with your international guests - before the meeting, in the taxi, at the airport or over a coffee.

Your main linguistic tool in successful small talk is the open question. Small talk is like a friendly game of tennis. The idea is to keep the ball going backwards and forwards over the net. This means the questions you ask should not just require a simple "Yes" or "No" answer. Use the "W" question words. What? Why? When? Where? Who? Which? hoW?

Asking open questions and inviting longer answers makes it easier to develop a conversation.

- *What would you like to see here during the visit?*
- *The Museum of Modern Art.*
- *Oh, why is that?*
- *There's a couple of Van Gogh's there I'd like to see.*
- *Which are those?*
- *Two views from the time he spent in Arles.*

Such questions open up the conversation and start the ball rolling.

Do remember to keep your end of the tennis game going even if you come from a culture where small talk is not important. Even when your partner asks you questions that you could answer with one word – don't. Answer with a sentence and then ask an open question of your own.

Remember:
- Build a platform of agreement.
- Use open questions.
- Keep the "tennis game" going.

The Prime Minister of a small European country was due to meet the President of the United States. He wanted to make a good first impression but his English was rather poor. He took some private lessons and concentrated on learning the greetings. His teacher told him that if the President said, "How are you?" that he should answer, "Fine thanks." And that he should then not forget to ask back, "And how are you?" The great day arrived, and the President shook his hand and said, "How are you Mr Prime Minister?" Nervous and a little overawed the Prime Minister replied, "Fine thanks." Just in time he remembered – ask back. His mind went blank. All his English vocabulary seemed to disappear. After a long pause he said, "And who are you?"

3. Look for "hot buttons"

We all have "hot buttons" – personal interests that are important to us. They might include family, travelling, sports, pets, hobbies etc. If someone gets us talking about our "hot buttons" we can talk for hours. Friendship is often based on two people having similar "hot buttons".

In international business look for your business partner's "hot buttons" and explore whether you have any "hot buttons" in common. Now how can you do this and when?

You need to be a "hot button" detective. People leave you clues in their conversations with you. When a business partner, in the coffee break, says, *"Did you see the game on television last night?"* it's another way of saying, *"Is football one of your hot buttons?"* When your business partner says, *"I hope we finish on time. I've got some tickets for the theatre this evening."* They are saying, *"Do you like the theatre?"* So, don't just say, *"Yes"* or *"I see"*. Follow it up like a good detective. Tell them you support Bayern Munich or Chelsea. Ask what play they are going to see. And then, most importantly, offer some information back. Say that you prefer rugby to football. Tell them you went to see a good film last week. The best way to find out someone's family situation is not to ask a direct question – *Are you married?"* the answer might be embarrassing – *"Actually my wife has just run off with my best friend and taken the kids"* Oops! Sorry I asked! Instead tell your partner that your wife and kids are away this week on holiday and that you will join them at the weekend. Then they can volunteer information about their family if they feel comfortable about it.

Explore possible common interests and in that way build up a relationship that is not purely based on the business. In some cultures this is imperative.

Test yourself:

What clue could you drop to get the following responses from a business partner?

Example:

Clue   *Will it be a late evening Friday? I have to get up early on Saturday for a game of golf.*

Response   *Oh do you play golf too?*

Clue   ....
....

Response   *I prefer white wine myself.*

Clue   ....
....

Response   *Two boys. I've just got the one girl.*

Clue   ....
....

Response   *Have you visited Sienna?*

There are many possible ways of doing this. You can find some models below.[5]

Remember:
- Be a "hot button" detective.
- Offer information about yourself.

_____

[5]a. I've just had a weekend break in France – sampling some red Bordeaux. b. Just had a text from my wife saying our two boys will be coming to Paris with their school in the summer. c. I think my favourite holiday was in Tuscany.

4. SOFTEN your approach

There are three key areas we need to think about when meeting our international business partners – what we say; how we say it; and how we act. But we are often so concentrated on the words we want to use and on their pronunciation and intonation that we forget the non-verbal side of the communication.

We need to **SOFTEN** our approach. Each of the letters in the word **SOFTEN** reminds us of an important non-verbal signal we should use in conversation.

S - Smile! A friendly face helps people feel welcome and more relaxed. Too often we forget to smile. We are concentrated on getting the language correct. Our facial expression becomes serious and our forehead creases up. We come across as critical, cool and unfriendly.

O - Open gestures. Sitting with arms and legs crossed can subconsciously affect our speaking partner. It may give the signal that we are closed to the relationship or closed to the other person's ideas. But often we do it because we are feeling defensive about working in English not because of the relationship with the other person. Gesture naturally and sit with your feet next to each other on the floor.

F - Forward lean. When we want to show interest in another person we lean forward. This is more noticeable when we are sitting down but also happens when standing in a "cocktail party" situation. It creates a positive "I'm with you" feeling.

T - Touch. Normally we only touch each other in business when we shake hands at the start of the meeting. But we read a lot into that handshake! If the handshake is too aggressive or of the "wet fish" variety, we judge people negatively. A good international handshake is firm – but not too firm – and lasts for two to three shakes.

E - Eye contact. This varies according to cultural background but, according to some studies, during the average European conversation:

- the listener looks at the speaker 75% of the time.
- the speaker looks at the listener 40% of the time
- they look each other in the eye 30% of the time
- the average length of mutual eye contact is 1.5 seconds

If we stare at each other without breaking eye contact, this is perceived as being aggressive. In fact, in some cultures the eyes are lowered during a conversation to show respect.

But in most cultures we need to reassure ourselves that someone is still listening – and we do that by eye contact. It's a way of getting feedback on how our ideas are being received.

N - Nod. Moving your head up and down to indicate agreement encourages your speaking partner to open up. Your nodding tells them that you are listening and that you want them to continue speaking.

These non-verbal signals work in any language but are even more important when you are working in a second language. They underline and reinforce the verbal messages and can help correct misunderstandings. If someone asks you where the toilets are and you point upwards but say, "Downstairs", they are more likely to believe the hand signal than the words.

Try this experiment with a friend. Ask him or her to tell you about their last holiday. While they are speaking use the **SOFTEN** approach to encourage them to talk. After a minute or so start to switch off the **SOFTEN** signals – stop smiling, cross your arms, lean back, push your chair back, look down or away and shake your head. Your friend will either stop talking or get irritated. Stop and then discuss how it felt. Both parties usually agree that the first minute was great but that it soon became tense and unpleasant. Some people get really mad at their "negative" listening partner. If that happens – apologize and blame this book

Remember:
Smile
Open gestures
Forward lean
Touch
Eye contact
Nod

People greet each other in different ways in different parts of the world. Eskimos rub noses. Maoris touch foreheads. Thais hold their hands in a prayer-like attitude. In Japan they bow and in Europe and the USA they shake hands. Sometimes we try to make the other person feel at home by greeting them in the way that is expected in their culture.

Then you might get the situation where the American bows to the Japanese whilst the Japanese holds out his hand to be shaken.

5. Grab opportunities

You are surrounded by opportunities to practice your socializing skills. You need to grab them with both hands.

Try "on-the-job" training. Look for opportunities to use English during your normal work activities or in breaks and "dead" periods. Here are a few tips and ideas you could choose from.

- Practice with English-speaking visitors

Whenever English speakers visit your organization take the chance to practice your English with them. Volunteer to take them to lunch. See it as an opportunity rather than an imposition.

- Find other English addicts

There are probably several of your colleagues who would also like to practice their English. Arrange a weekly "English only" lunch or coffee break – or even an English Pub Night every month.

- Find a native speaker coach

If you have a regular English-speaking contact on the phone or a native speaker colleague, try to build a friendly trainee-mentor relationship. Ask if you can check your language with them. Many native speakers like to become the "expert" and "coach".

- Attend international events

Think of trade fairs and road shows as chances to practice your networking skills in English as well as business opportunities. Go on business training programmes where you have to use English to communicate with the other trainees.

- Try practising in your spare-time.

Join an English-speaking organisation.

There are many "friendship" societies where you can meet people from other cultures and where English is the medium of communication. Organisations like the Columbus Society, the British Council and various embassies often hold events and lectures in English.

- Chat to English speakers when you are relaxed on holiday.

It's fun to meet new people and it's a safe environment for making and correcting mistakes.

- Small talk in English with your family.

Have some fun in English together. It helps to improve your children's and your partner's English too.

In other words, look for every chance to extend your personal and professional network in English. Every time you socialise successfully in English you are building your confidence and giving you the chance of doing it even more successfully the next time.

Remember:
- Take every opportunity to practice.
- Practice at work.
- Practice at home.

Telephoning

Someone once said, "You cannot not communicate." You don't have to say a word. People will simply interpret both you and your silence.

In fact, communication can be divided into three main areas – body language, para-linguistics (how you say it) and the actual words you use. An American study carried out by Professor Albert Mehrabian showed that the impact of any face-to-face message is broken down as follows:

> 60% - Body language
> 30% - Para-linguistics
> 10% - Words

This is good news for second language speakers. The non-verbal messages can compensate for lack of vocabulary and incorrect intonation. But when we are talking on the phone the 60% disappears and we have to rely on using the correct words and saying them in the correct way.

Tips 6 –10 can help you compensate for the missing 60%.

6. Preparing the call

The telephone is a strange instrument. It sometimes requires us to speak to someone we don't know, without seeing to whom we are talking.

This can be stressful especially if we are also making the call in a second language.

If the call is important it requires preparation. Take a large post-it and write in one sentence in English the main reason why you are calling. Then, if there are several reasons for the call, prioritise them under that sentence. It could read something like this:

Main reason: *To make an appointment with Michael Garner when I'm in Britain next week in order to demonstrate our new e-learning software for computer security.*

Other reason: *To check if his company still intends to attend the trade fair in Hanover in September.*

Now take another post-it and write down the things you want to happen as a result of the call. For example:

Actions

1. Michael gives me two hours on Wednesday afternoon or Thursday morning.

2. If they are going to Hanover, we arrange a dinner meeting during that week.

Think of a call you might have to make in the next few days. Practice by writing two post-its. See how well you can define your reasons for calling and the actions you want.

Now you need to think of the words you might need to use. Prepare your opening sentences so that you make a good first impression and practice them. If you are nervous, learn them by heart.

Good afternoon Mr Garner. This is Werner Kamitz from Interlearn Software in Germany. The reason I'm calling is to see if you are able to meet me when I'm in Britain next week. You sent us an email showing interest in our new computer security e-learning programme.

Then think through the main points of the call in English. Note any concepts where you can't find the right word. Afterwards look up the missing words, make a short vocabulary list and run the call through again in your head.

Try to put yourself in the shoes of the person receiving the call and think what questions he or she might ask and your answers to them.

This process is very good language practice. You could try it even when the call is not critical, simply to activate your English.

When you actually make the call place the two post-its where you can see them. Check you have relevant documents to hand and a pen and paper, of course. Have your list of key words in English to hand in case your mind goes blank at a critical time.

Make yourself comfortable. Pick up the phone and ring. When the person you want to speak to answers – smile. This makes your voice sound cheerful and friendlier. And usually you get a smile back. Say your name slowly and clearly. Then give your main reason for calling straight away to help focus the receiver on you and on the subject of the call.

Remember:
- Write down the reason for the call
- Prepare your opening sentences
- Put yourself in the receiver's shoes

When one of Albert Einstein's colleagues asked the eminent physicist for his telephone number one day, he reached for a telephone directory and looked it up. "You don't remember your own number?" the man asked, understandably startled. "No," Einstein replied with a shrug. "Why should I memorize something I can so easily get from a book?"

7. Answering a call
What's wrong with this telephone conversation?

Caller: Hello, this is Mark Thomas from Smithson and Co in London.
Receiver: Hello.
Caller: Is that the Sales Department?
Receiver: Yes, that's right.
Caller: Who am I speaking to please?
Receiver: Blom. I'm Mr Goldmann's Personal Assistant.
Caller: Could I speak to Mr Goldmann please?
Receiver: No, he's in a meeting all morning.
Caller: Then could you take a message for me please?
Receiver: Certainly.
Caller: Please tell Mr Goldmann we've had trouble with the shipment again – several faulty items.
Receiver: What was the shipment reference number?
Caller: 2376/67- 00.
Receiver: Good. I'll tell him and he will get back to you.
Caller: When can I expect his call.
Receiver: He'll be back in the office this afternoon.
Caller: So I can expect his call then?
Receiver: Of course.
Caller: Right, thank you.
Receiver: You're welcome. Goodbye.
Caller: Goodbye.

The secretary is efficient and does what is expected of her – but no more. She answers the caller, gives him whatever information he needs and gets rid of him as quickly as possible. Now sometimes we need to be short, sharp and effective. Sometimes we need to get rid of unwanted callers quickly. But usually we are interested in building business relationships and then the short, sharp approach is not at all appropriate. It could also be the personal style of the secretary to act in this way – but it's more likely to be her discomfort at talking in English on the phone.

Here are five rules when answering an international call in English:

1. Be proactive

Don't answer questions with just one or two words like *"Yes"* or *"No"*. And offer information or assistance – *"How can I help you?"* or *"Let's see what we can do to sort this out"*.

2. Empathise

If something has gone wrong or the caller is angry, show you understand their feelings – *"I understand how you must feel"* or *"I'm sorry to hear that"*.

3. Use the caller's name.

Our names are important to us. So get the caller's name and use it once or twice during the call to fix it in your memory. It also makes the caller feel better too.

4. Small talk

If it's appropriate, take the chance to make small talk. The caller feels you are friendly and interested in them. Listen for signals when they want to small talk too.

5. Smile

Remember that the only body language signal available to us on the phone is the smile. You can hear a smile. It helps create a positive, helpful approach.

Here's a better version of the call to Mr Goldmann:

Caller: Hello, this is Mark Thomas from Smithson and Co in London.
Receiver: Good morning Mr Thomas, this is Hannah Blom in Sales. How can I help you?
Caller: Could I speak to Mr Goldmann please?
Receiver: I'm afraid he's in a meeting all morning. But I'm his Personal Assistant, maybe I can help you.
Caller: Could you tell Mr Goldmann we've had trouble with the shipment again – several faulty items.
Receiver: Oh I'm very sorry to hear that Mr Thomas. Let's see what we can do to

put that right as quickly as possible.
Caller: Thank you.
Receiver: Do you have the shipment number there?
Caller: Yes, 2376/67-00
Receiver: 2376/67-00. I'll get the documents out for Mr Goldmann and get him to call you as soon as he comes back in. Will you be in your office this afternoon?
Caller: Yes, I've no intention of going anywhere in the rain we're having!
Receiver: Oh bad luck, it's a lovely day here!
Caller: Maybe I should move to Germany.
Receiver: Well it would make correcting the shipments easier!
Caller: That's true. So you'll see to this will you?
Receiver: Yes I will. And you can expect Mr Goldmann's call this afternoon.
Caller: Thanks for your help.
Receiver: You're welcome, bye.
Caller: Bye.

Remember:
- Be proactive
- Empathise
- Use the caller's name
- Small talk
- Smile

Thomas Edison coined the word "hello" (from halloo - the traditional call to rouse hunting dogs) as a casual greeting on the phone.
Graham Alexander Bell's preferred telephone greeting was the sailors' "Ahoy!"
Edison's phrase quickly became more popular.

8. Twenty key words

If you know these twenty words you will be able to discuss the process of phoning with an operator or secretary.

Test yourself and learn any of the words you failed to identify.

Put the correct word in the space in the text on the next page.

1. *area code*   2. *check*   3. *confirm*   4. *connects*   5. *country code*
6. *dial*   7. *directory*   8. *direct line*   9. *email address*   10. *hang up*
11. *inform*   12. *letter (of the alphabet)*   13. *look up*   14. *make an enquiry*   15. *make a note of*   16. *on behalf of*   17. *operator*   18. *reach*   19. *receiver*   20. *switchboard*

I want to --------- about prices in a hotel in the USA. I know the -------- for the United States and I have the number for the hotel, but I have to --------- the number for the -------- for that part of America. I can find it in the telephone -----. I pick up the -------- and --------- the number. I get through to the hotel's -------- and ask the -------- to help me. She -------- me to Reception. I tell the receptionist I am calling -------- of my company and that I want to ------- room prices and availability. I -------- of what I needed to know. She asks for my name and I have to spell each --------. She then asks for my phone number and whether I have a --------. I tell her on which number she can -------- me. Before I ------- I give her my -------- and ask her to ------- the prices and availability in writing. I am now going to ------ my colleagues about what I have found out.

Now check your answers in the footnotes[5]

Remember
- Learning these 20 telephone process words makes it easier to discuss what you want to do on the phone.

---

[5] I wanted to ----**14**----- about prices in a hotel in the USA. I knew the ----**5**---- for the United States and I had the number for the hotel but I had to ----**13**----- the number for the ----**1**---- for that part of America. I found it in the telephone ----**7**----.

I pick up the ----**19**---- and -----**6**---- the number. I get through to the hotel's ----**20**---- and ask the ----**17**---- to help me. She ---**4**----- me to Reception. I tell the receptionist I am calling ----**16**---- of my company and that I want to ----**2**--- room prices and availability. I ----**15**---- of what I needed to know. She asks for my name and I have to spell each ----**12**----. She then asks for my phone number and whether I have a ----**8**-----. I tell her on which number she could ---**18**----- me. Before I ---**10**---- I give her my ----**9**---- and ask her to ---**3**--- the prices and availability. I am now going to --**11**---- my colleagues about what I had found out.

9. Twenty key phrases

Here are twenty phrases to help you manage a telephone conversation.

Controlling the conversation:
Can you hold?
Could you repeat that please?
Could you speak more slowly please?
Could you speak up a bit please?
One moment please.
Sorry, I didn't catch that.
Sorry, I didn't get that

Spelling and names
Could you spell that please?
Is that "A" as in Alpha?
May I have your name please?
What was your name again please?

Dealing with difficulties
I'm afraid he's not available.
I'm afraid it's rather urgent.
I'm afraid there's no answer.
It's busy / engaged.
Sorry, we were cut off.
This is a bad line.

What you are going to do.
I'll call you back? I'll find out.
I'll transfer you.

Here are twelve telephone situations. Choose a phrase from the list to deal with each one appropriately.

1. You want the caller to wait for a few seconds.
2. The caller is speaking very quickly.
3. You want to tell the person you are calling that you need this dealt with quickly.
4. The person they want to speak to is not in the office.
5. You want the caller to tell you their telephone number again.
6. You didn't hear their name clearly.
7. You want to connect them to another colleague.
8. The caller's voice is very faint.
9. You don't understand what the caller is saying.
10. You are trying to put the caller through to a colleague but her phone just keeps on ringing.
11. You don't want to speak now but will return their call.
12. You want the caller to spell a word using a spelling alphabet.

Check your answers below.[6]

Remember:
- Learn any phrases you are not sure of and you will then sound professional when dealing with international calls.

The great British comedian Spike Milligan once telephoned an airline and was placed on hold while the dreaded "hold music" chimed in his ear. When he was finally put through to a human being, Milligan said: "Just a minute" - and proceeded to sing a whole chorus of "Hey Jude."

10. Dealing with difficult speakers
Speaking in a second language on the phone can be a frustrating business. At least when you are face-to-face you have the help of body language and facial expression to support the communication. But on the phone you are reduced to the words you use and how you say them. Ideally you want a caller who speaks slowly, clearly and to the point. Unfortunately, this is

---

[6] a – 1 or 5 b – 3 c – 13 d – 12 e – 2 f – 11 g – 20 h – 4 I – 6 or 7 j – 14 k – 18 l – 9

often not the case. Sometimes, if your caller is a native speaker, they speak much too quickly, use complex language and have a strong regional accent. Or, if your telephone partner is a weak English speaker, you have to deal with limited vocabulary and poor pronunciation.

How many times can you say to a caller that you haven't understood before it gets embarrassing? Sometimes we even agree to things on the phone, without understanding exactly what we have agreed to, simply because of this embarrassment.

As soon as you get into difficulties let your telephone partner know. Don't wait, hoping that things will become clearer later on – they rarely do. Here is a 5-stage linguistic tool to help you overcome this difficult situation.

Stage 1: - Interrupt by using the word *"Sorry?"*. This one word is enough. And your partner hardly notices that they have to repeat what they just said.

Stage 2: - You still don't understand. Now use another one-word interruption – *"Pardon?"*. Again, it's short and hardly noticed. (Don't say the same word twice – it's more noticeable.)

Stage 3: - This time it is noticeable if you still do not understand. Now you need to soften your interruption with some politeness, and you need to sound friendly. Use a sentence like – *"I'm afraid I still didn't quite catch that."* *"I'm afraid"* is polite – *"didn't catch that"* is colloquial and friendly – *"quite"* means that we're almost there, we only need to make a little more effort to succeed.

Stage 4: - You still don't understand. Now it's getting more difficult! This time you need to be proactive and guess what you think was said. It doesn't matter if you guess wrongly! - *"Oh! You mean Tuesday?"* What you want is for your partner to then correct you. This they usually do slowly and clearly. - *"No, I mean Thursday!"*

Stage 5: - If you still don't understand at this point, ask them to send a fax or email! And try to make a joke of the situation to keep it friendly.

Remember:
- Sorry?
- Pardon?
- I'm afraid I still didn't quite catch that.
- Oh! Do you mean …?

The bathtub was invented in 1850 and the telephone in 1875. In other words, if you had been living in 1850, you could have sat in the bathtub for 25 years without having to answer the phone.

Negotiations

"A miser and a liar bargain quickly."

Greek proverb

Tom Peters, the American management guru, says the key attributes of the successful negotiator are the willingness to take risks, the ability to think under stress, and stamina and patience!

Pierre Casse, in his book "Training for the Cross Cultural Mind", lists three key skills for the international negotiator. You should be able to see the world as others see it. You should be able to deal with ambiguous situations. And you should be able to express yourself so that everyone can understand.

This last skill is key for second language speakers. Tips 11 – 15 will help you improve your ability to negotiate clearly in English.

11. Be prepared

The scouts' motto is "Be Prepared". This is not only true for scouts. It's also absolutely necessary for international negotiators. If the negotiation is to be held in English then do the preparation in English. It might take you a little longer but you will soon discover any linguistic shortcomings. You will then have time to correct them.

Having clear goals for the outcome is vital. You need to ask yourself three basic questions:

What is the optimum result I want?

What is my "walk away" point?

What is my BATNA? – My Best Alternative to a Negotiated Agreement.

In other words, you need to decide what you hope to gain, the level where agreement becomes impossible and what alternative you have if the negotiation fails.

Write down the optimum result in English. Everything you do in the preparation and in the negotiation itself should lead towards achieving these goals.

Specify (in English) your absolute minimum requirements and what you would not be prepared to accept.

Now you can more easily see possible options for compromise between the two.

Decide clearly what you intend to do if the negotiation is unsuccessful. What are your other alternatives? Knowing you have a BATNA gives you strength in the negotiation.

Then you need to put yourself in the other side's shoes and ask yourself the same three questions. This way you can see where the potential areas of agreement are and the possible bottlenecks. Of course, these are assumptions you are making and you will need to check them. This you can do with tip number 12, the questioning funnel.

Don't forget to take into consideration the history of the relationship – has it been positive or negative so far? And what do you know about the cultural background of your negotiation partners? What's their level of English like?

If you make these preparations in English, it allows you to rehearse and practice the language you need in order to move the process along successfully. With your targets and arguments pre-prepared and clearly stated in the target language you can then concentrate on the negotiation process itself and on the other people rather than struggling to find the right words and arguments.

Failing to plan is planning to fail.

Remember:
- What is the optimum result I want?
- What is my "walk away" point?
- What is my BATNA? – My Best Alternative to a Negotiated Agreement.

12. Funnel your questions

In international negotiations it's very important to make sure that you check your preparation and assumptions before you start the hard bargaining. The questioning funnel is a practical tool to help you in this process, especially when someone is reluctant to give you the information you need.

Start your questioning process by asking open questions which are easy for your partner to answer. Then gradually move down the funnel. This process gradually opens up your partner until you find out the specific, hard facts that you were looking for.

The Questioning Funnel
Open
soft issues
attitudes, opinions, feelings,
context, relationships

General open questions

"What do you want to achieve in the future?"
"Why do you need this kind of service?"
"When did you begin manufacturing in this way?"
"Who are involved in this project on your side?"
"What's your opinion about the new materials?"
"How do you intend to market this?"

Framing questions

"How does this fit in with your other services?"
"How do you normally approve suppliers?"
"What would you do if delivery was delayed?"

"What if…." questions

"What have you done in this situation in the past?"
"What if the exchange rate goes down?"
"Why do you say that?"

Asking for evidence

"What makes you say that?"
"Are those the only reasons?"
"Did I understand you correctly when you said….?"

Checking questions

"So what you are saying is…."
"So what you mean is….?"
"How many items are you considering?"

Pushing questions

"How much would you think is a reasonable price?"
"When would you need this?"
"High quality? Can you specify that?"

Blockbuster questions

"A team of salespeople? how many exactly?"
Speedy delivery? Compared to what?

facts, figures, statistics
information
hard issues
Closed

You can also help this process along by asking *"Tell me more"* at any stage along the funnel. Silence is also a way of encouraging someone to add information to something they have said.

Remember:
- Start with open questions
- Closed questions for the facts
- "Tell me more"

A man goes into a lawyer's office. "How much do your services cost?" he asks.
"Ten thousand dollars to answer three questions." The lawyer replies.
"Isn't that rather expensive?" asks the man.
"Yes." Says the lawyer. "Now what's your final question?"

13. If...then

In most international negotiations we are looking for a "win-win" outcome. And successful negotiation depends on bargaining, with both sides making proposals and counter-proposals linked clearly to certain conditions.
"If you give us a 6% discount then we will sign the contract."
"If we made the delivery time shorter would you then agree to the other conditions?"
As competent international negotiators we need to be able to deal with the different kinds of conditional sentences in English so that we are able to send correct messages to our business partners. We have to make our own offers clear, understand what the other side is offering and indicate our level of acceptance or rejection of their offers.
Now there are many different types of conditional sentence in English – "If you had thought negotiating was easy then you wouldn't have bothered to learn how to use conditionals properly, would you?" But luckily many of them are not as complicated as that example! In fact, the good news about using conditionals in negotiating is that you only need three basic forms to cover most of what you need to say. Let's look at each of these in turn and the situations in which they may be used.
a) When you want to make a proposal which is likely or possible.

This is the most common use of the conditional and is easy to use.

"If you accept the new delivery terms then we will give you a 2% discount."

Use this conditional to signal to your partner that you think agreement is near and likely. (The most common mistake for second language speakers of English is to use the future *"will"* in the *"if"* part of the sentence – *"If you will accept then we will give you a 2% discount."*)

b) When you want to make a proposal which is less likely or improbable. You can also use this conditional to make a counter-proposal.

"If you gave us a 4% discount then we would accept the new delivery terms."

This gives the feeling that you think your negotiation partner will be more reluctant to accept this proposal. Or that you are offering this as a counter-proposal to an offer of theirs that you are not happy about.

(The mistake here is to put *"would"* in the *"if"* part of the sentence – *"If you would give us a 4% discount then we would accept the new delivery terms."*)

c) When you want to clearly show that an offer is unacceptable or when you are speculating about the past.

"If you had accepted a 3% discount then we would have agreed to the new delivery terms."

This conditional is used after the negotiation to show what might have happened. It is also used during a negotiation to reject a proposal whilst, at the same time, setting out your own conditions for agreement.

(The common mistake in this type of sentence is to put *"would have"* in both parts of the conditional.)

Perhaps the most quoted use of the conditional in English is when Winston Churchill was approached by a female political opponent who said, "Mr Churchill, if you were my husband, I would put poison in your tea." To which, Winston Churchill replied," Madam, if you were my wife, I would drink it!"

Remember:

- Probable - "If you accept the new delivery terms then we will give you a 2% discount."

- Improbable - "If you gave us a 4% discount then we would accept the new delivery terms."

- Impossible - "If you had accepted a 3% discount then we would have agreed to the new delivery terms."

"Compromise" is not a dirty word.

14. Recognise hidden signals

"We will never agree to what you are proposing" is a clear statement of position. But if you add the words *"in its present form"* you immediately indicate the possibility of a negotiated agreement.

Giving and understanding these kinds of signals are all part of the skill of negotiating. But reading between the lines in this way can be a problem for a second language speaker. What exactly do your native-speaker negotiation partners mean when they say, *"We would find it extremely difficult to meet that deadline"*?

Basically, it is a question of listening between the lines. Listening for words that make definite statements more tentative and listening for statements which only rule out one of the possible alternatives. *"Extremely difficult"* is not the same as *"impossible"*. And maybe *"that deadline"* could be negotiated too.

Here are some examples:

1) *"We never negotiate on price!"*

This sounds very definite, but the hidden signal is that they would happily discuss delivery, quality and quantities.

2) *"These are our standard contract terms."*

The implication is that there are also non-standard terms available.

3) *"We could not produce those quantities in that time-frame."*

But they are prepared to negotiate either the quantities or the times.

4) *"Our price for that quantity is $40 000."*

Different quantity, different price!

5) *"These are extremely reasonable conditions we propose."*

This is the position they prefer but it's negotiable.

Here are five more sentences with hidden signals. What is the possibility for negotiation?

a) It is not our normal practice to pay within 30 days.

b) We never give discounts of more than 5%.

c) We are not prepared to discuss this now.
d) Our production line is not set up to deal with these requirements.
e) I am not empowered to negotiate these levels of discount.
You can check your answers in the footnotes[7].

There are also hidden signals of another kind. Some cultures prefer to make difficulties and differences of opinion less obvious than they really are. They do this for reasons of politeness and to imply that all problems can be solved.
"We have a bit of a problem with this." This can mean that the problem is a considerable one.

Here are some other examples:
"There's a short delay in production."
Check the exact timing.
"I have some doubts about the project."
How many are *"some"*?
"There seems to be a slight misunderstanding."
This is often used as a serious warning of difficulties.
"We just need a little more time."
Try to get your business partners to specify how much more time they need.

In some cultures people understate difficulties in order to keep the business relationship harmonious. It is not usually a deliberate attempt to hide the truth. But be aware that soft words can sometimes hide deep disagreement.

Remember:
- Listen for tentative words
- Listen for what's not said
- Listen for politeness qualifiers

---

[7] a) So who's normal? It's negotiable. b) Never say never! And 1% - 5% are negotiable anyway. c) But we are prepared to discuss it later. d) So let's negotiate the alternative requirements or the costs of re-setting the production line. e) Take me to your boss!

An older gentleman had serious hearing problems for a number of years. He went to the doctor and the doctor was able to have him fitted for a hearing aid that allowed the gentleman to hear 100%. A month later he returned to the to the doctor and the doctor said, "Your hearing is perfect. Your family must be really pleased that you can hear again." "Oh, I haven't told my family yet." the gentleman said. "I just sit around and listen to the conversations. I've changed my will three times!"

15. Use silence

A Japanese teacher of Shintaido, a philosophy connected with body movement, once said to me that the British and Americans have forgotten that silence is communication. He had recently been giving workshops in Scandinavia where, he said, they still knew the art of being silent.

In our modern international business lives, we are surrounded by a sea of noise from people and machines. We get used to it. But at the same time, we know that silence can be a powerful and effective tool in our communication.

In most European business situations up to five seconds of silence is perceived as allowing you to gather your thoughts. Up to twenty seconds of silence is seen as encouraging you to continue speaking and adding to what you've already said. Over twenty seconds is perceived as pressurising you to make a confidential confession – as used in police interrogations!

So, silence is a key listening skill. It shows our speaking partner that we are concentrating on what they are saying. It gives them time to think. It encourages them to continue. In negotiations or interviews, if we remain silent, our negotiation partner or interviewee will often add to the information they have already given us. And in the case of the negotiation they might well give us just that piece of information we need in order to judge whether a deal is possible.

Saying nothing can be as powerful as saying something. It can imply that you feel secure in what you are doing and create a feeling of uncertainty in your business partner. If you have made a clear proposal say, "So, what do you think?" - and then sit back and wait. This often has the effect of forcing a concession from the other side.

Silence is also a useful tool when presenting your ideas. If you pause before part of your message your business partner automatically sharpens his or her attention. If you pause after a statement, this underlines the importance of what you have just said.

Remember:
- Use silence to show you are listening
- Use silence to encourage your partner to add information
- Use silence to emphasise your ideas

"Remember that silence is sometimes the best answer."
Dalai Lama

Presentations

A couple of years ago Fortune Magazine ran an article about the hidden fears and phobias of top managers in the USA. They discovered that the number one fear - above fear of snakes, heights, loneliness, sickness or death – was giving presentations!

The main reason was that people who have to present are often frightened that they will make a fool of themselves in front of others. And they are worried that their personal and professional credibility will suffer.

When you have to make a presentation in a second language this puts even more pressure on you as a presenter. Tips 16 –20 will help you relieve some of that pressure. Wherever giving presentations in English is on your personal list of fears and phobias, these tips will help to push it even further down.

The famous Shakespearean actor Sir Laurence Olivier was once asked if he felt nervous before a performance. He replied that all good actors should feel some butterflies in the stomach before going on stage as this gave the performance energy. He then went on to say that the main difference between good actors and great actors is that the great actors can make their butterflies fly in formation.

16. Open with impact

Most international business presentations seem to start in the same way – "Good morning ladies and gentlemen, I'm very happy to be here today and to have been given this opportunity of speaking to you all. I'm afraid that thirty minutes is too short a time to deal with this complex subject, but I'll try to cover as much as I can." We've all heard this hundreds of times before. It's boring, predictable and has no impact. We all know what's coming and we're only half listening. But many second language speakers of English follow this safe, conventional approach because they don't know what to do instead.

For me the start of any presentation is a key success factor. We need to wake our audience up, to focus their attention on us and on our subject and to motivate them to listen carefully. And this is especially true when presenting to British or American audiences.

So how can we improve our impact in the first thirty seconds of our presentation?

There are three key "Don'ts" and three key "Do's".

The Don'ts

1) Don't start with greetings and clichés – "Good morning ladies and gentlemen, I'm very happy to be here…".

If you want to greet the audience or thank them for coming, wait until you've grabbed their attention and shown clearly the purpose of your talk.

2) Don't over-use the word "I" – "I'm very happy to…", "I'm afraid...", "I'll try to…".

"I" is a distancing word. It separates you from your audience and makes you sound self-centred.

3) Don't start by apologising – "...thirty minutes is too short a time to deal with…" or start by being negative – "...I'll try to cover as much as I can." What you are doing is telling your audience that it isn't really worth their while listening to you.

The Do's

1) Do start with a powerful first sentence. Here are some examples:

- *"Improving our after-sales service is vital for our future success."*

(This is a "subject heading" start, similar to a headline on a letter or report.)

- *"Why do we need to improve our after-sales service?"*

(This is a rhetorical question that forces your audience to think about your subject.)

"At the end of the next thirty minutes we should all be aware of the reasons why we need to improve our after-sales service."

(This is an initial benefit promise, which motivates your audience to keep listening.)

2) Do include your audience in your presentation by using "we" and "you".

Instead of saying - *"I want to show you how to deal with this problem"*, say – *"So, how should we deal with this problem?"*.

Instead of saying – *"The next picture summarises what I've been saying"*, say – *"The next picture summarises what we've been discussing"*.

Instead of saying – *"I think we should do the following…"*, say – *"Let's do the following…"*.

3) Do be positive and motivating in your approach.

- *"In the next thirty minutes we'll cover the five main issues."*
- *"Imagine that we have increased sales by 20% and are now number one in our market."*

Learn your first five to ten sentences by heart so that you can concentrate on sounding confident to your audience.

According to many psychologists we only have thirty seconds to make a first impression. Make sure the first impression you make on your international audience is a positive one.

Remember:
- No clichés but a powerful first sentence
- Avoid "I" and include the audience
- No apologies - be positive

An American businessman had to speak to a mixed audience – half were from the States and half were Japanese. How could he open with impact when there was such a cultural mix?

This is what he said.

"I'm told that in Japan you should start a presentation with an apology. In America we usually start with a joke.

Ladies and gentlemen, I apologise for not starting with a joke today."

17. Signpost clearly

Have you ever been to a "Christopher Columbus" presentation? This is where the presenter, like the famous explorer, starts off not knowing where he's going, doesn't know where he is when he arrives and isn't sure where he's been when the journey ends!

When you are speaking to an international audience with different linguistic and cultural backgrounds you have to have a clear, logical structure to the presentation. And you have to help your audience by sign-posting the route you are taking.

What then is the best structure for a presentation? There is the well-known 3-step structure – *"First of all tell them what you're going to tell them, then tell them and finally tell them you told them!"* In other words, start by giving an overview of what you are going to cover, then go through it point by point and finally summarise your main ideas.

Let's take each step in turn.

Step 1 – "Tell them what you are going to tell them."

Firstly, grab the audience's attention with a good opening. Then motivate them by telling them what they're going to get out of listening to you. And finally explain the process and main points you intend to cover.

For example:

"Why should we all be learning and improving our English? At the end of this 45-minute presentation you will understand the importance of using International English and will have some simple tools to help you improve your own English language skills.

Firstly, we'll discuss what International English actually is and why we should use it. Then we look at three areas where most second language speakers need improvement and, finally, we'll look at some simple tools for self-improvement."

Step 2 – "Then tell them."

Go through the main points of your presentation one by one. Make sure the flow is logical and that you clearly signal when you are moving from one point to another. This is what I mean by "sign-posting." Often, we have a good, logical structure to our presentation but forget to, or are not able to make this structure transparent to the audience.

"So now we understand the importance of using International English when you are communicating with people from different cultural backgrounds.

Let's go on now to look at the three main improvement areas for second language speakers.

Firstly, we need to identify "false friends" and start the process of getting rid of them."

You can practice the skill of sign-posting by doing the short exercise on the opposite page.

Remember that we often over-kill our audiences with too much detail. So make sure you only have three to five main points in the main body of your presentation. More is too many!

Step 3 – "Tell them what you told them."

If you want your audience to remember what you said the next day – make a clear summary of your key messages. If you can, choose the three most important ones. This allows the audience to easily grasp them and it allows you to build your summary up into a proper climax.

"To summarise. Using International English allows us to communicate clearly and on an equal basis with both native and second language speakers.

Ridding our language of false friends, confusing grammar and poor pronunciation will make us feel more confident in using the language.

And finally, using the tools we discussed, we only need to spend ten minutes a day to become a more proficient international English speaker."

Think of your next international presentation as a piece of music and you as the conductor. Firstly, introduce the main theme. Then elaborate on the theme in different ways with different instruments. Finally bring the piece to a close by a memorable crescendo – ending on a high note!

Sign-posting exercise
Fill in the blanks in the short presentation on the next page with the 10 words or phrases below.

to sum up	firstly
secondly	let us now turn
this means	finally
during	on the contrary
on the other hand	as you may know

There are three key groups we need to take care of – and the first of those is the customer, the second is the customer and the third is the customer!

…..1….. the next five minutes I will outline three reasons why we need to re-focus on our customer care programme.

…..2….. we know that a dissatisfied customer never buys from us again. …..3….. if we address the customer's complaints 90% will stay as our customers. ……4….. front-line staff have to be given the right to deal

immediately with such complaints.

.....5..... *we need to give the customer added value. This needn't be very expensive for us. .....6....., it might simply mean staff following up sales more quickly with a phone call.*

.....7..... *we need to train our staff more frequently and decide on a clear customer focus policy. .....8..... we have a team working on a proposal for this.*

.....9....., *we need to improve and update our customer care approach.*

.....10..... *to the future. I propose we spend the next 30 minutes making a short action plan which we can present to the management.* [8]

Remember:
- First tell them what you are going to tell them
- Then tell them
- Then tell them you told them

18. Put yourself in your audience's shoes

It was once said that there are three key things you need to think about in order to make sure your presentation is a good one. The first is the audience – and the second is the audience and the third is – the audience! They are the reason you are there. So, in order to make your presentation a successful one you need to define and assess who your audience are and try to put yourself in their shoes. To do that you need to think about five things and to help me remember them when I'm preparing a presentation, I use the acronym **MEETS**.

M means Motivation.
Why are your audience there? Why should they be listening to you? Do they really want to be there? You might have a lot of good ideas but are they relevant to this particular group of people? Are your audience fresh or are they suffering from jet-lag? Often people are there simply because it's the weekly meeting or because their boss told them to be there. If people are not particularly motivated, you have to provide that motivation.

---

[8] 1 – During 2 – Firstly 3 – On the other hand 4 – This means 5 – Secondly 6 – On the contrary 7 – Finally 8 – As you may know 9 – To sum up 10 – Let us now turn

But if people are highly motivated for particular reasons then you need to address those reasons.

E means Expectations

Most audiences have certain expectations. Are they expecting to be informed, entertained, amused, convinced, challenged or bored? Whenever someone in an audience is listening to you, they are also mentally tuning in to an internal radio station – WIIFM – What's In It For Me? Somewhere along the line you need to give an audience what it needs or expects. Occasionally you might need to change the unrealistic expectations of some audiences or deliberately upset their expectations in order to create an impact.

E means Experience

What does your audience already know? This can be their level of knowledge of the subject area and their previous experience of you, your organisation, your products or services. Has this previous experience been positive or negative? What is the cultural and linguistic background of your audience? In other words, on which level do you need to pitch your message?

T means Time

How long do you have for the presentation? Most presentations suffer because the presenter tries to cram too much information into too short a time. You need to plan your material to fit the time limits and your audience's ability to take in the information. The worst thing you can do is to tell an audience you are going to speak for 20 minutes and then go over time to 30 or 40 minutes.

S means Size

How many people will you be speaking to? There is nothing worse than expecting to speak to ten people and finding yourself facing 100! With smaller audiences it can be easier to establish relationships rapidly, be less formal and create a workshop atmosphere. With audiences of ten or more it's usually better to stand up and it requires a more formal presentation style. Larger audiences (over 30 people) are more anonymous and more demanding. The larger the audience, the more theatrical the situation. You then really need to think carefully about your visual aids, lighting, projecting your voice or using a microphone and how to run question and answer sessions.

Use the **MEETS** approach before preparing any presentation you make. It might only take a few minutes with groups you know well whilst it might take much longer with groups you have never spoken to before. Then you might have to really do some homework, make some calls to conference organisers, to some of your prospective audience or to colleagues who know them.

Remember the saying "Proper Preparation Prevents Poor Performance." Putting yourself in the shoes of the audience will start that preparation off in the right way.

An example of a **MEETS** audience assessment for a presentation on Time Management in a workshop at a conference for middle managers.

Motivation

As the participants have signed up for this part of the conference, they should be fairly motivated. Some of them seem to be fellow trainers who want to get some new ideas but most of them are genuine managers who want to learn either for themselves or to pass on to their own staff. Check this at the start of the presentation.

Expectations

The advertising for the presentation emphasises that they will gain some practical tools for their working situations. They probably expect 4-5 tools they can take away and use immediately. As the workshop is at the end of the afternoon, they need to be kept awake! Build in activation exercises.

Experience

Most of them have almost certainly some experience of time management techniques otherwise they would not be managers or trainers. Try to check this with the conference organisers. Choose to present the more creative, less standard tools for this group.

Time

60 minutes. Rather short time so don't have a question and answer session at the end – the interactive approach should allow for their questions to be answered during the process. Maximum four tools – 15 minutes each.

Size

So far 12 people have signed up and the maximum allowed is 30. The organisers think probably 20 will turn up. So, this will be a stand-up, more formal presentation.

19. Handle the difficult questions

The most difficult part of making a presentation in a second language is not the presentation itself. It's the question and answer session at the end. You can carefully prepare and rehearse the actual presentation but you are never quite sure what questions will be asked.

Remember that people ask questions for a variety of reasons and not only as a genuine request for further information. Often, they want to impress the rest of the audience or their boss with their own knowledge of the subject. Or they want to test you to see if they can knock you off balance. But however aggressive the questioning, the golden rule is to never react in an emotional way yourself or you will have "lost the game".

So, what can you do if someone asks a question and you are not sure what they mean? Or if someone asks a question and you are not sure of the answer.

Keep control

As presenter you are in authority. Do not surrender this automatic authority to someone else. Act like the chairperson in a meeting. Take time to think of your answers but then be firm in your replies – no hesitancy. Keep eye contact with the whole audience during your answer not only with the questioner. This prevents a dialogue situation from occurring. And if you are expecting strong reactions to your presentation, give a clear agenda at the beginning making it clear you will only take answers at the end. This prevents your logical flow from being interrupted and allows you to put all your arguments on the table before the questions start.

Clarify complicated questions

There are several ways of dealing with this situation. First of all, say that you are not sure you have understood the question and then: -

a) Ask the questioner to repeat the question.

"I'm not sure I understood that. Could you repeat the question please?"

b) Ask the questioner to explain the question in another way.

"I'm afraid I didn't get that. Could you explain what you mean exactly?"

c) Try to paraphrase the question.

"If I understand you correctly what you are saying is…"

Admit you don't know the answer

Never try to bluff the audience into thinking you know the answer to a question. You will be found out. But there are several positive things you can do in this situation.

Say that you don't know the answer and then: -

a) Promise to find out the answer later.

"I'm afraid I don't know the answer to your question right now, but I'll find out and let you know tomorrow. Is that OK?"

b) Refer to an absent expert colleague.

"I'm not sure about the answer but my colleague Mr Kent is an expert in this area. I'll ask him to contact you tomorrow. Is that OK?"

In both situations get the agreement of the questioner on the procedure you suggest and then carry out your promise!

c) Throw the question back to the questioner.

"I don't know, but what's your experience in this?"

Often the questioners know the answer to their own questions and are only too happy to have the chance to show off their knowledge.

d) Throw the question open

"I don't have the answer but does anyone in the audience have any experience in this area?"

In most audiences there are people with considerable experience who can help you.

Use humour

Humour always makes an audience more sympathetic to your situation as presenter.

"Thank you, Mike. I was hoping no-one would ask me that – trust you to ask the one thing I don't know!"

But it must be successful and appropriate. It normally only works if you know your audience or are totally confident that what you are saying is amusing and relevant.

Finally, if you have nothing more to say, say nothing! Ambrose Bierce the American writer and journalist said, "A bore is a person who talks when you wish him to listen." Don't be a bore.

Remember:
- Keep control
- Clarify complicated questions
- Admit you don't know
- Use humour

George Bernard Shaw was not only a brilliant author, playwright and wit. He was also an excellent public speaker. People turned up in their hundreds to hear him speak. On one occasion, after a superb speech, the audience stood and cheered for minutes on end. Just as the noise was subsiding a man at the back suddenly started to shout, "Boo! Rubbish! Boo!" There was a short, embarrassed silence before George Bernard Shaw leant forward, peered at the back of the room and said," Sir, I agree with you. But what can we two do against so many!"

20. Manage your ending
"So, ladies and gentlemen, I'd just like to say once again that I'm sorry Mike Jones was unable to talk to you this evening and I apologise for the fact that I didn't have the time to prepare myself as well as I should, even if I did take over at short notice but I do hope you feel you have got something out of this little talk anyway. That's about it I think. Oh, does anyone have any questions?..........No? Fine, I must have managed to explain myself fairly clearly. Thank you for your attention."
Too frequently the last words we hear in business presentations are unmemorable, lacking in impact and full of platitudes. This example of a bad ending breaks 5 golden rules for closing international presentations!
1) Don't apologise – end on a positive feeling not a weak, negative feeling. Now sometimes you need to apologise – for turning up late for example. Then you need to make a sincere apology earlier in the presentation. But don't include this apologetic feeling in your final message.
2) KISS – keep your final sentences short and simple. This makes them easier to understand and more memorable. The first sentence in the example contains about 70 words. It should be broken up into at least four shorter sentences.
3) Don't undermine your own professional status with phrases like "I hope", "this little talk" or "I think". These weaken your message by giving the impression that what you are not sure of the importance of what you

are saying.

4) Don't end with the words "Thank you." This simply indicates that your final sentence is not strong enough and that you have to tell your audience that you have ended! The "thank you" is more for your sake than your audience's. If you really do wish to thank the audience, do it earlier in the presentation and it is less likely to sound like a cliché.

5) Don't end by asking for questions. If you do, you run the risk of giving the final word to your questioners. And when you do ask for questions remember it is more positive to ask for "some questions" rather than "any questions". "Some" indicates you expect a positive response.

So how should you end your presentation?

Your ending should include a summary of the main points of your talk. If you can do this with just three key messages, this makes your ending easier to remember and allows you build up to a climax.

Ask for questions before you summarise. That way you can deal with any difficult questions and then take back control for your final message.

Pause before your ending; change your voice, emphasis and speed. Make it clear to your audience that this is important for them.

Learn your last five or six sentences by heart. This allows you to concentrate on your audience and on how you are saying the words rather than concentrating on what to say.

Finally, say the final sentence with emphasis, pause slightly and then leave centre stage to prevent your key messages being diluted by one more question!

"So before we summarise, are there some questions?.....(deals with questions).....Do you have some more? .....No?.....So let's just summarise the three key points we've discussed:

Firstly, sales targets need to be more realistic. Secondly, customer care training needs to be available for all after-sales personnel. And, finally, the sales force needs to be reorganised to meet the demands of a changing market-place."

Remember:
- 3-point summary
- Pause and change your voice
- Say your final sentence with emphasis

Writing e-mails

Writing is a system of inscribed signs replacing or recording spoken language.
From A Dictionary of World History

"Miss Walther, could you take a letter please?" Up until just a few years ago a secretary was expected to write all outgoing letters, memos, reports and messages. Shorthand and the ability to use the dictaphone were seen as key secretarial skills. But the advent of fax and now e-mail has changed priorities. Many secretaries have now taken on the role of "personal assistant" or "executive secretary" with their own projects and areas of responsibility. And managers are now expected to be computer literate and communicate both internally and externally by e-mail. Writing skills have become more important. Tips 21 – 25 will help you improve your English e-mails.

Easy reading is damned hard writing.
Anonymous

21. KISS your writing

Sometimes I start an English seminar by saying that the key to international communication is how well you KISS! After the initial surprise, most of the participants realise that I don't mean kissing in the romantic sense but rather KISS in the communication sense – Keep It Short and Simple – or as our American friends might say – Keep It Simple Stupid!

KISSing in English doesn't necessarily save you time when writing, as you need to edit and refine the message. But it certainly saves the time of your reader. And when you are speaking, KISSing has two effects. Firstly, you are more easily understood, not only by native speakers but also by weaker second language speakers. Secondly, it's easier for you to construct short, simple sentences in your head rather than long, complex ones.

KISSing can also create impact for your messages whether written or spoken. For example, in his inaugural speech, John F Kennedy could have said,

"We are endeavouring to create a more inclusive society." He didn't. Instead he KISSed the message to give it greater impact and the result was this - "We are going to make a country where no-one is left out." Similarly, Winston Churchill at the time of Dunkirk could have said, "The position with regard to France is a cause of some considerable concern but we are convinced that the end result will be favourable to Britain." But he didn't. He said, "The news from France is very bad. We are sure that in the end all will come right."

So, what are the rules for KISSing in English?

1) Short words.

Test your KISSing technique with the short test below. Look for the common, easy, simple words first and only use longer, less frequent words if you need a synonym for stylistic reasons.

Find one short word for the following words or phrases.
1) commence
2) in the near future
3) terminate
4) due to the fact that
5) in the event of
6) approximately
7) purchase
8) Request
9) Dispatch
10) with reference to

Check your answers at the bottom of the page[9]

2) Short sentences.

There should be one thought in each sentence. For two thoughts use two sentences. Many writers in English, however, love long sentences with several sub-clauses and lots of commas. But when you are writing, "pepper your page with periods". In other words, put full stops instead of commas

---

[9] 1) start 2) soon / ASAP 3) end 4) because 5) if 6) about 7) buy 8) ask
9) send 10) about

and make your sentences shorter but varied in length. Remember that a sentence with more than 20 words is difficult for the reader. According to writing experts the best average length of any sentence is only fifteen words. Generally, aim for sentences of between 8 and 18 words.

Don't write – *Kindly dispatch the goods at your earliest convenience?*

Write – *Please send the goods ASAP.*

Gustav Flaubert was once asked the reason for his success as a writer and replied as follows: -

> Whenever you can shorten a sentence do.
> And one always can.
> The best sentence?
> The shortest.

Try shortening the following sentence.

> *The form enclosed with this letter is from the Accounts Department who would like you to complete it in full, attach your signature and return it to us at your earliest convenience.*

You can find a model answer in the footnote.[10]

3) Short paragraphs

Each paragraph should contain one "unit of thought". But it should not be too long. A page is much more reader-friendly if it has a lot of white space.

Remember:

Short words

Short sentences

Short paragraphs

> *George Bernard Shaw once ended a twelve-page letter to a friend with the following:*
> *PS I apologise for the length of this letter, as I had no time to write a short one.*

---

[10] *Please complete and return the enclosed form by 31 August.*

22. Learn netiquette

When you are working internationally, in English, are there any rules for writing e-mails? Some people say that an e-mail is just the same as a face-to-face conversation, so the style of writing is unimportant. I disagree. When we meet socially, we follow some unwritten rules of behaviour called "etiquette", so that we don't upset or insult each other unnecessarily. In the same way there are certain rules we need to follow when e-mailing each other – "netiquette"!

Here are five simple rules for international, business e-mails.

1) Don't e-mail anything you would not send on company headed notepaper. An e-mail might be less formal than a letter, but it is still an official communication on behalf of your organisation.

2) Be polite - especially if you are asking for something. This helps show respect for your international partners and guards against being perceived in some cultures as too direct or aggressive. Use "would" instead of "will", "could" instead of "can" and put "please" at the end of the sentence rather than in the middle.

"Could you let me have the figures by Friday please?" is much more acceptable to the reader than "Can you please let me have the figures by Friday?" As a rough guide, ask yourself "Would I say this to the person face-to-face?"

3) Always fill in the subject box. This focuses your reader's attention and allows him or her to file your mails properly.

4) Never put anything you would not put on a postcard. Remember e-mail is often copied and re-distributed. Also inter-net connections are not confidential. Even e-mail you thought you had deleted can often be recovered.

5) Avoid capitals.

THEY MAKE YOU LOOK AS IF YOU ARE SHOUTING!

If you want to be sure that the emotional content of your e-mail has been interpreted correctly you can always use "emoticons" – symbols made up from the keyboard. The most common one is the smiley face : -) to show you are feeling happy. But what are these emoticons on the next page?

1   :- (

2   ;-)

3   :- o

4   :- ( )

5   %- (

6   :`- (

7   :- /

8   ***

9   [ ]

Check the answers below[11]

Remember:
E-mails are still official
Be polite
KISS it
An e-mail is like a postcard
Don't use capitals

23. Write with impact

You have 15 seconds to show your reader what your document is about and why they should read it. If you need to write emails, faxes or letters in English here are six golden rules to help you keep your reader's attention.
a. Put your main ideas first.
Don't keep your readers waiting for the key idea. Tell them first and then follow up with background and details.

---

[11] 1 – frown or sadness 2 – wink showing a joke 3 – shocked 4 – can't stop talking 5 – confused
6 – crying 7 – not sure 8 – kisses 9 - hugs

The department needs to replace the existing copier with a new print-on- demand machine.
The present copier does print quickly enough, and it is difficult to maintain. A new print-on –demand machine copies at a much higher speed and is more reliable. It also has several printing features that would make our documents look more professional.

b. Know your readers.

Are they familiar with the subject? How much do they know already? What are they expecting to hear? What do you want them to do afterwards? Will other people read the document?

c. Be reader-friendly.

Put yourself in the reader's shoes and look at your document through their eyes. Use headlines in different print for emphasis and numbering or lettering to make the division of ideas clear. Repeat important ideas to show their importance. Put details and background figures in a separate enclosure. Information overload is the main reason for people not taking in your main messages.

d. Make the mail visually attractive.

Leave plenty of white space – especially around key ideas. It's so much easier to read on the screen.

Each paragraph should contain only one main idea. Never write a paragraph that contains more than 100 words – your reader switches off after that. A densely written text stops many people even starting to read it. Would diagrams or pictures show the information more clearly?

You could write this:

When you come to us next week you can find us more easily if you drive along the High St from the West (or walk from the station) past the first two roads on your left. Then take the third road (Lime Walk) on the left and continue up to the traffic lights where you turn right into Lee Drive. We're number 43 on the left.

But why not attach a simple map instead or refer the reader to your website if there are directions for visitors?

e. Use active rather than passive sentences.

Don't write: *A new chairperson was chosen for the meeting.*

Write – *The meeting chose a new chairperson.*

f. Try not to start sentences with *"It is…"* or *"There is…"*. The subject of your sentence should be clear.

Don't write – *There were five people at the meeting.*

Write – *Five people were at the meeting.*

Lee Iacocca the former CEO at Ford and Chrysler once wrote, *"The discipline you use to write things down clearly is the first step in making them real."* So, make sure that what you write today helps make what you want tomorrow a reality.

Remember:
Main items first
Know your readers
Reader friendly
Visually attractive
Active not passive
Clear subject of the sentence

The shortest correspondence on record was supposedly between Alexander Dumas and his editor. Dumas sent in the sequel to "The Three Musketeers". He heard nothing for several weeks. Finally, he sent a note to his editor:

Dear Sir
  ?
Yours
Alexander Dumas

The editor, who disliked the new book, replied:

Dear Alexander
  !
Yours etc

24. Know the conventions
1. Should you use "I" or "we" when writing on behalf of the company? It depends on the situation and purpose of the correspondence.

Use *"I"* when you are really speaking for yourself or when you take personal responsibility for something.

"I will mail you the figures you need on Monday."

"I'm sorry I was unable to return your call last week."

Use *"We"*, *"Us"* or *"Our"* when you are describing what your organisation does, expects or needs.

"We are manufacturers of microchips."

"Our suppliers know our needs exactly."

"Please send us the goods by Friday."

"We" can mean the company, your department or you and your reader. If there is a chance of misunderstanding be specific.

"In Sales we need better contact with Customer Service."

"You and I need clearer guidelines from our accountants."

Do remember that both *"I"* and *"We"* distance you from your reader. Use them sparingly. Try instead to turn your sentences into *"You"* sentences which are much more reader friendly. Instead of writing *"We would like you to visit us soon."*- write *"You are welcome to visit us soon."*

2.What's the best way to write the date?

You see the date written in several different ways:

2009 – 02 – 06	0 6/02/09	2009-06-02
February 4th, 2009	4th Feb 2009	

I would recommend you do not use any of the above. The versions in the first line are confusing internationally. It's not always clear which is the month, and which is the day. As for the two versions on the second line it's no longer necessary to write the *"th"*, *"st"* or *"rd"*.

If you want your date to be clearly understandable, I would write the month out in full and separate the day from the year as follows –

4 February 2003. Now there can be no chance of misunderstanding.

3. If you don't know the name of the person you are writing to how should you start and end the mail?

Try to avoid writing to someone when you don't know his or her name. People tend to ignore correspondence if it is not addressed to them personally. But if you really have to write such a mail then I would use:

Dear Sir/Madam and sign off with *Yours faithfully.* This follows the standard conventions for official correspondence.

With most emails you nearly always have a name but are sometimes not sure of the gender of your reader. Then I would use the whole name – *Dear Chris Hadow.*

If you do know the gender of your reader use the titles *Mr* for a man and *Ms* for a woman in your first mail. In some cultures you can go over to first names on the second mail while it may take longer in others.

You can end mails with rather informal salutations such as *Regards, Best wishes, Kind regards* or *Yours.*

4. Is it acceptable to use well known abbreviations like *e.g.* / *i.e.* / *ASAP* / *etc.* / *PS*?

Generally speaking I would avoid these abbreviations in formal letters and when mailing other second language speakers. In the first instance abbreviations affect the formality of the letter and in the second instance they may be misunderstood. So, unless you are mailing a native speaker write them out in full –

for example / in other words / as soon as possible / and so on.

PS – Post Script- is unnecessary in this world of computers where it's very easy to insert additions to your text.

5. How should you sign a letter or mail on behalf of someone else?

There are three ways to sign on behalf of another person.

You can write above or beside the name and title of the person for whom you are signing the words *"for"*, *"on behalf of"* or the letters *"pp"*.

For example:

> *Ken Taylor*
> *pp* Michael Jones
> Purchasing Manager

Correct the following email.

Dear Mr Michael Jones

Thank you for your mail dated 03 – 04 – 21. Could you also mail us the name of your colleague who I will be meeting tomorrow? I need this ASAP, as I will be leaving at two o'clock this afternoon.

Don't forget that John Kent my Head of Purchasing is expecting you on the 3rd of May as previously arranged.

See you soon

Yours faithfully
Brian Garner
Check with our model answer.[12]

> *Only a mediocre writer is always at his best.*
> W. Somerset Maugham

25. E-mail exercises

1. Look at the last five e-mails you wrote in English. Check the number of words in each sentence. For every sentence with 18 or more words there should be 4 sentences with fewer than 18 words. If a sentence has more than 18 words, the meaning may become "foggy" to the reader. Now try to make those long sentences into two shorter sentences by putting in a full stop.

2. Now read your five e-mails aloud. After each one, ask yourself if you would actually say this to the person face-to-face. And ask yourself how you would feel if someone said this to you. Because e-mails are less formal than official letters it's sometimes easy to come across as rude or abrupt.

3. Check the subject box at the top of each e-mail. Does what you have written fully reflect the contents? The subject box helps the reader focus on the key message or messages. This really assists fellow second-language speakers.

4. Find an English language "e-mail pal" (remember the "pen-pals" from school?). Send each other an e-mail every second week telling each other what you have been doing since the last mail. You can do this with a German friend or colleague or with an English speaker who wants to improve their German. In the latter case you write in English and they write in German.

---

[12] *Dear Mr Jones (or Dear Michael)*
Thank you for your mail dated 21 April 03.
Could you also send me the name of your colleague who I will be meeting tomorrow? I need this urgently (as soon as possible) as I will be leaving at 2 o'clock this afternoon.
Don't forget that John Kent our Head of Purchasing is expecting you on 3 May as previously arranged.
See you soon.
Best regards
Brian Garner

5. Read each e-mail you receive in English on two levels. Firstly, read it to extract the meaning in order to be able to act on it in your work. Secondly read it critically from a linguistic / communicative point of view. Ask yourself what you would have changed to make the e-mail more reader-friendly.

Remember:
Check the "fog factor"
Read aloud
Check the subject box
Find an e-mail "pal"
Read received e-mails critically

"I don't give a damn for a man that can only spell a word one way."

Mark Twain

Meetings

"People who love meetings should not be in charge of anything."
Thomas Sowell (Stanford University)

International meetings can be difficult because linguistic and cultural differences often exaggerate the business differences. Then if the meeting is
not well organised and run, it can be chaotic and very time-consuming.
Yet meetings are often the tool we use to get decisions made and to spread
information. Many of us spend many hours a week in meetings. So how
can we ensure that this time is not wasted when working internationally?
Tips 26 – 30 deal with improving your meeting skills in English.

26. Use the agenda

It is very important to prepare the meeting properly. And the main tool to
help in that process is the agenda. There are two things you should con-
sider when creating an agenda:
Firstly, carry out all your agenda discussions and preparations in English.
This allows you to practice the vocabulary you need to take part in the
meeting. It also means that you will identify those areas where you are
missing words and give you the chance to look them up.
Secondly make sure the agenda is a well thought out logical tool that helps
the participants to understand the purpose of each item.
Have a look at the agenda below and decide whether it's good or not: -

AMCO International
European Sales Meeting
16 May 2---
1) Introduction
2) Reports
3) This year's sales targets
4) New products
5) Recruitment
6) Any Other Business

It's not very good, is it? An agenda has to fulfil four main criteria to help the chair steer the meeting through its business: -

- It should communicate the purpose of the meeting and the and the goal of each item.
- It should include necessary practical information.
- It should have a logical order of items.
- The language should be clear and concise

Here's a better version:

AMCO International
Quarterly European Sales Meeting
Agenda

To be held on 16 May 2--- between 09.00 and 12.00 in Conference Room D (Where and when)
Participants: Mr T Jones (Chair), Ms A Heimbring (Secretary), Mr F Lacroix, Ms G van Eyl, Mr D Ponti, Mr G Evans. (Who should come)

1) Apologies (Those who can't come and why)
2) Minutes of previous meeting (To check if they were written correctly)
3) Progress reports from each subsidiary (Information) (15 minutes each x 4 = 40 minutes) (What kind of discussion and for how long?)
4) Revision of sales targets for 2--- (Decision - 30 minutes)
5) Strategy for introduction of new products – Amcolite and Amcorex (Decision - 40 minutes)
6) Staffing requirements for 2--- (Preliminary decision - 30 minutes)
7) Any Other Business
   (15 minutes) (Only very urgent items permitted here)
8) Date of next meeting (While everyone is there with their diaries)

As you can see this example is fuller and clearer. The participants know what they have to prepare and why they have to prepare it. The practical information, including timings, looks more professional and helps the

Chair move the meeting along. A good agenda also helps the meeting's secretary with the minutes afterwards.

It's the responsibility of the Chair to write the agenda in consultation with the participants. It's also the responsibility of the Chair to make sure the agenda is circulated at the appropriate time before the meeting together with any background papers. This is good business practice in any language but when the meeting is being held in a second language the preparation usually takes that bit longer.

As far as the language is concerned it's important to get the correct balance between simplicity and content. It should be clear what each item is about. For example if you write *"Item 5 – internal communication"* – what does that mean? It could be about email systems or frequency of meetings or the company newsletter or the use of staff mobile phones. The item on the agenda should clearly define the issue to be prepared and discussed – *"Item 5 – Increasing the number of European Sales Meetings to six each year."*

Finally, if you are the Chair, one tip – make sure the first 30% of the meeting is spent discussing easy items where there is little chance of strong disagreement. This allows the participants to warm up their English in a comfortable atmosphere and creates a feeling of cooperation before dealing with the more controversial or difficult items.

Remember
Hold your agenda preparation discussions in English
Balance clarity with simplicity
Put some easy items first

27. Learn 15 key words

It helps enormously if you have the right words and phrases to describe meeting procedures. These words and phrases support you in keeping control of what's going on in the meeting and in writing the official follow up documentation.

There are about fifteen common meeting words and phrases you need. You should know them. They are useful in both formal and informal meetings.

Test yourself on the next page.

Match the words with the correct explanation.

Vocabulary	Explanations
1. agenda	a. A suggestion for discussion
2. calls to order	b. All the matters dealt with in the meeting
3. minutes	c. When the chair gets the attention of the members
4. A. O. B. (Any Other Business)	d. One point for discussion
5. adjourn	e. The person who runs the meeting
6. consensus	f. The written follow-up to a meeting
7. proposal	g. The list of points to be discussed
8. amendment	h. Action points from a previous meeting
9. item	i. The point where you can discuss subjects not listed in advance.
10. draft	j. Not according to the rules of the meeting.
11. second	k. A general feeling of agreement
12. out of order	l. To support someone else's ideas
13. chair	m. An early version of written ideas
14. business	n. A change to a proposal or document
15. matters arising	o. To close or end the meeting

How did you get on?[13]

With these fifteen words you've made a good start.

Remember

If there were any words or phrases you didn't know or were not sure about – learn them if you take part in meetings in English. At least make sure you understand them passively so that you know what native speakers are talking about.

A secretary runs in to her boss after hearing that Charles Lindberg has succeeded in his solo flight across the Atlantic. "Have you heard? A man has flown across the Atlantic on his own!" she cries.

"There's no need to get so excited," says her boss. "Most things can be done by someone on their own. Interrupt me when a committee meeting manages to fly the Atlantic – then I'll be impressed!

---

[13] *Answers:*

1 – g 2 – c 3 – f 4 – i 5 – o 6 – k 7 – a 8 – n
9 – d 10 – m 11 – l 12 – j 13 - e 14 – b 15 – h

28. Make yourself heard

We have a saying in English when we find it impossible to interrupt a speaker who is talking too quickly or without pausing. We say, *"I couldn't get a word in edgeways."* In other words, there were no gaps for me to take part in the communication.

Many business people who have English as a second language have the problem of making themselves heard over insensitive native speakers or other second language speakers who are highly fluent. We are often too concerned about linguistic correctness and sit working out what we want to say. By the time we have the correct grammatical construction and the right vocabulary, the meeting has changed the subject. We are now left with a "perfect" English sentence in our heads, which is now "perfectly" useless!

So how can we "get a word in edgeways" in international meetings? Native speakers often have an unconscious strategy for doing this and we can learn from it and adapt to our needs. It is called the **INSET** approach.

I -Interrupt clearly

Raise your hand, lean forward and use one or more of the following phrases *"Excuse me"* or *"Sorry, but..."*

"Could I just interrupt here?"

"Could I butt in here?"

"If I could just say something here."

Remember that in meetings in the Anglo-Saxon business world people accept being interrupted more readily than in the German business context and are more likely to interrupt you.

N –Need to think

Give yourself time. Use a filler phrase like –

"Now let me see."

"So, what is the question here?"

"How shall I put this?"

This allows you to collect your thoughts without having to have worked out exactly what you wanted to say before interrupting.

S -Show the context

Define the subject area clearly.

"It's mainly a question of..."

"We should concentrate on ..."
"The main point here is..."
> You need to focus your listeners and prepare them to listen carefully
> *To* your key messages.

E -Explain your proposal / opinion
> State your thoughts clearly in simple language so that you do not
> hesitate too much.
> *"I think we need to..."*
> *"I suggest that...."*
> *"My proposal would be to..."*
> *"Why don't we...?"*
> Hesitation may allow someone else to interrupt you or give the
> meeting the feeling you are not sure of your opinion.

T -Test agreement
> Try to see if there is a consensus on your views to save discussion time.
> *"Do you agree?"*
> *"Could you agree on that?"*
> *"Wouldn't you agree?"*
> *"Does this make sense?"*

Using the **INSET** approach we can more easily take part in the spontaneous interaction that international meetings demand. It's been said that there are three kinds of people in the world – those who make things happen, those who watch things happen and those who say, "What happened?" Let's make sure we "make things happen" in our next international meeting.

Remember
Interrupt clearly
Need to think
Show the context
Explain your proposal / opinion
Test agreement

*To get something done a meeting should consist of three people – two
of whom are absent.*

29. Summarise

A recent survey of companies and organisations in Europe reported that
only 40% of all decisions taken in meetings are actually carried out. This
confirms the old saying, "When all is said and done, there is usually more
said than done!"

Meeting participants need to understand what's going on in the meeting itself and should know clearly what it is they are expected to do after the
meeting. This can be difficult if the meeting is an international one – with
people with different language levels, cultural backgrounds and decision-
making styles.

One of the key linguistic tools the chair of an international meeting needs,
is the skill of summarising clearly and simply. Summaries are used for several purposes:

- to confirm exactly what has been decided

*"So, to summarise, we've agreed that Michael will send out the   invitations to the
kick-off meeting by October 2."*

- to check understanding

*"If I've understood you correctly, you're saying that the project has been delayed for
three weeks – is that right?"*

- to check the understanding of the participants

*"I'll just summarise at this point to make sure we're all clear where our discussion
is going. First….."*

- to signal the end of one phase of a discussion

*"What we've said so far is that there are two possible approaches to dealing with
the problem. First….."*

- to judge the degree of agreement

*"Do we have a consensus here for investing in the new equipment? If we do, then
all we need to decide are the amounts involved."*

- to signal to a participant that they have had enough time to speak

*"John, if I could interrupt you here, what you've been saying is that we need to in-
crease our fees by 5% - right? Any comments from anyone else?"*

- to help the secretary write accurate minutes

"Point 7 on the agenda. It was agreed that the Annual Sales Conference be post-poned until the week beginning June 6. This was to allow staff to attend the exhibi-tion in Hanover in May."

In international meetings it's a very good idea to summarise at regular intervals.

Summarising involves three skills:

1) Listen attentively – listen especially to the words people emphasise and underline with their voice. Listen to the intentions as well as the words. Check these intentions when you summarise

"So, when you say you disagree with the proposal, it's not just the money you are talking about but the feeling of mistrust – have I got that right?

2) Check understanding – when people use a second language, they often choose inappropriate words and sound more antagonistic than they intend

"Sven, you say that one of the problems we need to discuss is the increase in pro-duction. Do you actually see this as a problem or is it simply a practical question to be dealt with?"

3) KISS your summary – keep it short and simple. Use short sentences. Then if you have left something out it's easier for the other participants to notice it and for you then to add it to your summary.

Remember
Summarise frequently.
Listen carefully and check understanding.
Keep your summaries short.

A priest, a psychologist and a businessman are to face the firing squad.
They are allowed to decide themselves in which order they should be
shot. The priest says that they need time to pray and to contemplate the
after-life. The psychologist discusses how to deal with the stress of the
situation. After five minutes the businessman calls out to the captain
of the firing squad, "Shoot me first. I can't stand another damn busi-
ness meeting!"

30. Build a safety net

Many of us now work in international project teams or regularly meet international clients, customers and colleagues. The work of these meetings and project groups can be seriously held up if we are not prepared to take into account the way these meetings are run.

In any meeting – but especially in a meeting where language and cultural differences are present – we need to balance the "what" with the "how". In other words, we not only need to deal with the contents of the meeting, but we also need to think carefully about the process involved.

We want our international team to work well together and any international meeting to be effective. A good first step is to create a "safety net" in order to help all the participants feel comfortable with the way of working together.

There are six simple steps involved in this process.

1. Everyone should reflect on what they need to trust the group and the process.
2. Each person writes these needs on cards – one idea per card. The needs should be expressed in behaviours eg *"You should not interrupt another person" "No side conversations in a language the others don't understand" "There should always be a clear agenda"*
3. These cards are then stuck up on a wall or board and discussed for understanding. The person who wrote the card explains anything which is not clear.
4. The cards with a similar message are grouped into clusters. The group decides on a rule or rules based on the clusters.
5. The group then decides on the key points that could act as the rules for their team or for the meeting.
6. The rules are posted up in the room on a large sheet of paper.

What are the advantages of using up valuable meeting time on this process? Firstly, it makes the participants aware that there are different ways of working together and different needs within the group. Secondly it creates discussion around cultural differences which might get in the way of the work later. Thirdly it allows the linguistically weaker members to remind the more fluent speakers of the need to be considerate. Fourthly it reminds everyone that the success of meetings depends on a process which is acceptable to everyone.

Finally, it provides a set of rules or guidelines that can be pointed to by any participant when they feel the meeting is not working well.

One international legal company with its HQ in Britain regularly holds meetings where four or five nationalities are present. A "safety net" rule they have implemented is the "C spot"! Whenever a meeting member is not sure what is happening because of language, procedure or cultural confusion they raise their hand and say "C spot!" Whoever is running the meeting has the duty to address the problem and sort out any difficulties to that participant's satisfaction.

Other organisations always include a meeting feedback session at the end of any international meeting when everyone answers four simple questions:

- How was the atmosphere of the meeting in general?
- Did you feel you were able to participate fully? If not, why not?
- Was the chair effective? If not, why not?
- Did the meeting achieve its aims?

Most high-wire circus artists use a safety net to catch them when they make a mistake. In international meetings mistakes will occur regularly. So put a safety net in place to prevent those mistakes from fatally affecting relationships.

An example of a "Safety Net" for an international meeting.
We agree to:

1. Indicate immediately if we do not understand something.
2. Not talk over each other
3. Be linguistically democratic – that is allow space for less fluent speakers to have their say
4. Remember that all participants are cultural resources
5. Follow the chair or facilitator's rulings

We expect the chair or facilitator to:

6. Always have a clear agenda and minutes
7. Control side conversations especially if they are in another language (unless this is for agreed explanations for clarity)
8. Summarise at regular intervals
9. Monitor time effectively
10. Have a "scribe" to keep a written summary on a flip-chart

Reading business texts

"If you can read this – thank a teacher!"
Anonymous

How much time do you have for reading for pleasure? And how much of that time do you spend reading in English?

Many of us have the ambition to improve our English by regularly reading books and magazines, only to find that we have more pressing reading demands placed on us from work. We have to read in English but it's certainly not for pleasure. Instead we have to quickly try to pull out the key, relevant facts from a report written in technical, scientific, financial or administrative English. Here we are not concerned with language improvement but simply with reading efficiency in our second language. Maybe if we could be more effective in dealing with this kind of reading, we would be able to set aside more time for reading for pleasure!

Here are five tips on how to read in a more effective and business-like way in English.

31. Try rapid reading

Imagine you have been sent a 10,000-word report in English. You know that reading it from cover to cover would take you all day and that all you need are some key facts and conclusions which you want to refer to in a meeting. How do you go about it?

1. Read the title of the report and any sub-titles. This usually tells you the basic aims of the author – why it was written.
2. Read any introduction or forward, which gives you the context in which the report was written.
3. Now look for an executive summary. If the report writer is at all professional in their approach this should be at the start of the report. It gives you an overview of the main contents and recommendations. From this you can often see which parts are relevant to your needs. Otherwise you might find them at the end of the report or in the appendices.

4. Look at the chapter index. From this you can tell where those relevant parts are within the report. Go to those chapters first.
5. Read the first paragraph (which often outlines the contents of the chapter) and the last paragraph (which often outlines the main conclusions)
6. Now skim through the chapter paragraph by paragraph reading the first line of each. This frequently gives you a clear overview of the logical process the report writer is using and homes in on the information you need.
7. With long paragraphs that seem important to you, let your eye wander diagonally from top left to bottom right looking for words or phrases that seem relevant.
8. Read intensively those key sentences and paragraphs you identify as important. This means looking up any words you are not sure of and really making sure you understand everything in that passage.
9. Make notes as you go along and / or use a highlighter to indicate the important points.
10. Don't allow yourself to get tied down in details. Put a bookmarker in any place where you feel this is happening and go on to the next item. When you go back to this you will often find that information you have discovered later will help you understand the difficult passages.

You can go on rapid reading courses if you really want to increase your reading speed. But by just following these simple, practical tips you can increase the speed at which you gather the information you need. Which will then allow you that extra bit of time to read for fun!

Remember:
Look for short cuts
Read selectively
Don't get tied down by details

"I am not a speed -reader. I am a speed understander."
Isaac Asimov.

32. A 10-minute warm-up exercise

Reading quickly in a second language is very challenging. Here's a short warm up exercise that you can do at regular intervals. It will help you to stop translating as you read and to read groups of words rather than single ones.

Start with some easy reading material the first time and when you have done this exercise a few times, move on to more complex reading material. Do not look up any words that you do not know. Try to get the meaning from the context or just go on to the next sentence.

1. Read for one minute at a speed with which you feel comfortable and where you have good comprehension of what you are reading.
2. Mark where you have reached after one minute.
3. Add a third of a page to what you have already read and make a new mark.
4. Now go back to the beginning and read the passage and the new third of a page (still for good comprehension) in one minute.
5. Do this a couple of times until you are comfortable reaching the second mark in one minute.
6. Now add another third of a page and make a new mark. Read to this third mark in one minute. Do this a couple of times.
7. Add another third of a page and read to the fourth mark in one minute. Do this a couple of times.
8. Finally add another third of a page and make your fifth and final mark. Read to this mark in one minute.

You will realise that you are now not reading word for word but simply skimming the page. This is the point of the exercise. This will help you to recognise and read more than one word at a time.

Remember:
Have some fun doing this.
Reward yourself after reaching each of the marks.
Treat it as a game or a challenge.

"While the extra step of translation bars access to the highest reading speed, it will not prevent bilingual students from reading, comprehending, and learning faster."
Howard Stephen Berg, Guinness Book of Records "World's Fastest Reader"

33. Use newspapers as a learning tool

If you want to keep your English up to date and practice your reading skills, buy a British or American daily newspaper occasionally. Newspapers use modern vocabulary and expressions aimed at native speakers. Start by choosing one of the more serious papers such as The Times or the Guardian from the UK or the Washington Post or Herald Tribune from the US. Tabloid newspapers such as The Sun in the UK are filled with idioms, slang and national pop culture references which often make them more difficult to understand. Try one of these papers later.

Now have some linguistic fun with the paper you've chosen. Set yourself five tasks.

1. Skim through the whole paper and try to decide what kind of readership the paper is aimed at attracting - which social class, educational background, gender or political leanings? The paper's editorial will give you some clues and so will the type of adverts you can see. See also if there is a readers' letter page. If you are not sure about your conclusions, check with a native speaker.

2. Check if there are any references to your country and if so in what context. If there are reports on current events see what opinions are expressed. Decide if you think the reporting is fair.

3. Look at some of the headlines and work out what the stories are about. This can sometimes be more difficult than you think as many papers use double meanings of words in their headlines. Then check by skimming through the article just to get the main ideas. Test yourself with the exercise opposite.

4. Find a political or current affairs cartoon and see if you can understand to which event it refers. Usually it is something that is in the news and referred to somewhere in the paper.

5. Choose a short article that looks interesting and read it intensively. This means looking up every word you do not understand and being prepared to summarise it orally to a friend.

Doing this kind of linguistic exercise is especially useful just before travelling to the part of the world where the paper is published. It gives you an idea as to what is going on there and what people might be talking about. It can also offer you some cross-cultural insights, which could be useful in your business. In fact, many countries have an English language daily paper. In the James Bond books, 007 often buys the local paper when he arrives at some exotic location just to get a feeling for the place. (He also tries the local drinks before going back to his vodka-martini "shaken not stirred" – which is also not a bad idea!)

Try matching the short summaries of newspaper articles with the appropriate headline.

Summaries

1. Mobile phones are getting smaller and smaller with more and more functions.
2. Funeral workers are out on strike for better wages.
3. Policemen need to be fitter and lose weight in order to be effective in their work.
4. There aren't enough golf courses for the number of people who want to play in the London area
5. Dentists' fees are increasing more than the rate of inflation.
6. Not enough women are joining the armed forces as they think they will suffer from sexual harassment

Headlines

a. Missing Links
b. This May Hurt a Little!
c. Small Talk is Big.
d. It Won't Make a Man out of You
e. A Grave Problem
f. The Fat Blue Line

Now check your answers in the footnotes.[14]

Finally, if you are reading a British newspaper, the following well known, fun definitions should help you with task number 1.

The Times is read by the people who run the country.

The Daily Mail is read by the wives of the people who run the country.

The Financial Times is read by the people who own the country.

The Daily Telegraph is read by people who think the country should be run as it was 100 years ago.

The Daily Express is read by those who think it still is.

The Sun is read by those who don't care who runs the country as long as she has a stunning figure!

"I read the newspaper avidly. It is my one form of continuous fiction."

Aneurin Bevan

34. Reading from a screen

A great deal of our business reading is from a screen. This puts an additional strain on your eyes and on your English comprehension.

First three tips to help reduce the strain on your eyes so that you feel less stressed when having to read emails or their attachments in English.

- Change the font type or size to make life easier for yourself. You get used to certain font types and changing a document to a familiar type can make the reading less stressful. Enlarging the size can help too.
- Be careful with light. Natural light is often uneven and moves as the sun shifts across the sky. If you want to concentrate on a bright day, blinds help enormously. And avoid having the screen directly in front of the window – the light contrast may be too great.
- Avoid distractors on the screen. If you want to concentrate don't keep your desktop icons on display. Besides being distracting this will also have the effect of making the reading area smaller. Only have on the screen the work you are doing.

There are also three things you can do to help you read more quickly from the screen.

---

[14] 1 – c 2 – e 3 – f 4 – a 5 – b 6 – d

- Use the cursor arrow as a pacing device to help you concentrate. It helps you focus on what you are reading allowing your eyes to jump about the page and prevents you losing your place. Move it down the centre of the page line by line or in an S shape across each paragraph.
- Narrow the margins and use single spacing. It's often easier to take in the information when there are only a few words to the line. It's also easier then to read the information in blocks of words rather one by one. Double or triple spacing is a lot slower to read. S,o change any texts to single spaced lines.
- Scroll down rather than using the page down key. Scrolling can also help you to pace your reading and you no longer waste time trying to find your place after the page jumps.

Reading from a screen is very tiring and stressful. And when that reading is in a second language it creates even more stress. So, take frequent breaks if it is a long text. By reading effectively you will more than make up for the time you lose.

Remember
Prevent straining your eyes
Use the technology to help you read quickly
Take breaks

"The wonderful thing about a book, in contrast to a computer-screen, is that you can take it to bed with you."

Daniel J Boorstin

35. Practice makes perfect
The best way to improve any skill is to practice it. Your guitar playing will never improve if you don't practice the chords regularly. And your skills quickly become rusty if you don't practice regularly. It's the same with your reading in English. Here are some ideas to help you improve.
- Have fun
  Reading is time consuming. This means you need to be motivated to prioritise the time you need. So, read for enjoyment as well as for

your work. If you enjoyed the first two Harry Potter books in your own language – read the third one in English. If you like crime stories with a dark edge of realism – read Henning Mankell in the English translation. One tip - before buying a book open it up and read a page from the middle. This gives you an idea of whether the language level is appropriate and whether you like the author's style.

- Find your reading material
  And it's not only books you can read. There are hundreds of periodicals, newspapers and magazines you can read too. If you have a very specific interest – golf, travel, motor sports, knitting, football, wine etc – there is almost certainly a periodical which deals with your area of interest. Surf the internet and download articles of interest. Look up book reviews in Amazon.co.uk. Be a reading detective – find what you like and then read, read, read.

- Read regularly
  The more regularly you read the more you increase your passive vocabulary. Regular readers find they spend less and less time looking up unfamiliar words. Set aside times for reading for pleasure – the train ride to work, the flight each month to Geneva or the hour on Sunday morning when the kids are playing football. Subscribe to a specialist magazine or a magazine aimed at second language speakers such as Business Spotlight.

- Read intensively
  Take a short article from a magazine and read it thoroughly – looking up any words you don't know. Study the vocabulary list you compile. Make sure you understand every sentence. Then summarise the article in 100 words in English.

- Read extensively
  Take another article and read it without looking up any words or stopping to think about specific meanings. In other words, read the article to get out the main message. The first couple of sentences usually give you an idea of the context and by keeping the context in mind you'll be surprised how much you can pick up even when there are some sentences, phrases or words that are unfamiliar.

- Read critically
  Find a short article about a controversial subject. At the end of each paragraph ask yourself two questions – Did I fully understand the message? Do I agree with what the author is saying? In other words, don't just read English to practice your understanding but also read the English article as critically as you would one in your own language.
- Have two dictionaries
  If you are a serious student of English, you need a good translation dictionary and a good English – English dictionary. This second dictionary should be designed for students of English and not only have explanations of words but also examples of how the words are used in a sentence e.g. The Oxford Advanced Learners Dictionary of Current English.
- Use the dictionaries
  Whenever you look up a word in your dictionary make a pencil mark next to the entry. If you ever need to look up this word again – you need to learn it. Look up the word to get the translation first, then look up the word in your English – English dictionary and see how it should be used in English.
- Have fun
  I know I've already said this – but motivation is the key to reading success. So, make sure you read and make sure you enjoy it!

Remember
Have fun reading
Read intensively and extensively
Have even more fun reading!

"Reading is to the mind what exercise is to the body"
Joseph Addison

Listening

"We have two ears and one mouth so that we can listen twice as much as we speak."

Epictetus (c. 50-120)
Roman Stoic philosopher, former slave & tutor of Marcus Aurelius

As small children we first of all learn to listen, then to speak, then to read and, finally, to write. In our daily life we spend, on average, 45% of the time listening, 30% of our time speaking, 15% reading and only 10% of our time writing. So why is it that we often learn a second language by spending a large proportion of the time writing and reading? And we are rarely taught the skills involved in how to listen properly.

Listening attentively is a skill we all need in when communicating in our mother tongue. But it's especially important when we are working in a second language. It's then we really need to feel confident that we have heard and understood correctly. In our first language we often take this for granted. Tips 36 – 40 will help your listening and understanding skills in English.

"You know, it's at times like this when I'm trapped in a Vogon airlock with a man from Betelgeuse and about to die of asphyxiation in deep space that I really wish I'd listened to what my mother told me when I was young!"
"Why, what did she tell you?"
"I don't know, I didn't listen!"

Douglas Adams (Hitchhikers' Guide to the Galaxy)

36. Be a good listener
In his book "50 Activities for Unblocking Organisational Communication" Dave Francis lists eight main characteristics of a good listener:
1) Comfortable body position
Talking to someone who is sitting on the edge of their chair or who is fidgeting the whole time is almost impossible. You need to relax to listen properly and to give the right signals to your speaking partner.

2) Quiet and attentive

Too many interruptions can break the speaker's train of thought and give the feeling that you want to take over the conversation.

3) Keeps eye contact

Some statistics from Michael Argyle show that during the average European conversation the listener looks at the speaker 75% of the time. The speaker will only look at the listener 40% of the time. This is partly because the listener is trying to show interest and also because by looking at the face of the speaker and especially at the mouth, the listener can more easily understand what is being said. (The speaker can also see when your eyes glaze over from boredom or lack of comprehension!)

4) Shows interest

We do this by nodding our heads or by using encouraging sounds, words or phrases like – *"Mmmhm"*, *"I see"*, *"Right"*, *"I understand"*, *"Really!"*, *"Oh I know"*…etc. These signals tell our partner that we have understood and want them to continue.

5) Allows silence

A silence of up to 5 seconds or so allows the other person to collect their thoughts. If you jump in too quickly you may be interrupting a key message. A longer silence can become oppressive and pressurize your partner.

6) Asks questions to check understanding

"What did you mean when you said…?"

"When was that?"

"Why did he go there?"

The questions should be relevant and move the conversation along. Not only does the listener check their understanding, it is also another way of expressing interest.

7) Avoids jumping to conclusions

Some quick thinkers occasionally finish your sentences off for you. This is not only rude it also means they run the risk of putting their words into your mouth. So, try not to make judgements or jump to conclusions before the other person has finished what they want to say. By giving your partner the space they need to complete a train of thought, it also gives you the time you need in order to ensure you've understood everything.

8) Summarise

When working in a second language summarise regularly to make sure you are still on track – *"So what you are saying is..."* *"So if I've understood you correctly..."* These short summaries are useful for both conversation partners – the speaker can correct any misunderstandings whilst the listener feels reassured.

Remember:
Comfortable position
Quiet and attentive
Eye contact
Show interest
Allow silence
Ask questions
Don't jump to conclusions
Summarise

Listen!

When I ask you to listen to me
And you start giving advice,
You have not done what I asked.
When I ask you to listen to me
And you begin to tell me why I shouldn't feel that way,
You're trampling on my feelings.
When I ask you to listen to me
And you feel you have to do something to solve my problems,
You have failed me, strange as that may seem.
Listen!
All I ask was that you listen, not talk or do.
Just hear me.

Anon.

37. Control the conversation
Keep control of any conversation by using three simple language tools. First – don't be afraid to interrupt immediately if you are not sure you have

understood something.

Read this short extract from a telephone call and see how Mikael interrupts and controls the conversation with Paul.

P: So why don't we meet on the thirteenth to discuss this…
M: Excuse me Paul, did you say the thirteenth or the thirtieth?
P: The thirteenth. And we could check if Mark, Helga and mmmmmmmm could come too.
M: Just a moment Paul – what was the third name?
P: John
M: Right.
P: Perhaps we could meet in mmmmm this time and …
M: Sorry? I didn't get that.
P: In Manchester – it's easier for the other three.

Firstly, "Excuse me", "Just a moment" and "Sorry?" are very common ways of interrupting. It's important to interrupt as soon as possible if you haven't understood in order to keep control of the call.

The three interruption phrases are interchangeable although "Excuse me" sounds slightly more formal than the other two.

Secondly - use special phrases to slow people down, to clarify understanding and to say what you think.

Could you take it a little more slowly please? – when someone is speaking too quickly.

Could you speak a bit more clearly please? – I'm Hungarian – when they have a difficult accent or dialect.

I'm afraid I didn't get that. – when you haven't understood.

I'm afraid I didn't catch that. – when you didn't hear what was said.

Can I just come in here? – when you want to say something yourself.

What did you mean when you said….? – when the speaker uses a word you didn't know.

Thirdly - Make short summaries at regular intervals in order to confirm understanding and agreement. For example:

Native speaker: We have to go over the purchasing needs for the next three months.

So we need a meeting as soon as possible.
You: Let's meet next week then.
Native speaker: If we could meet next Monday it would be better for me –
preferably sometime in the afternoon.
You: I'm afraid that would be a bit difficult – I'm in a meeting all morning and
have an appointment at three as well.
Native speaker: How about the Wednesday? I'm free all day.
You: Great. I'm free from one o'clock. Could you come over here to me?
Native speaker: Sure and I'll bring the relevant papers.
You: So we'll meet next Wednesday at one o'clock in my office to go through the
purchasing needs for the next three months – right?
Native speaker: Right.

Summarising allow you to move the conversation along whilst, at the same time, also checking understanding. And you should always summarise all the main points you've discussed right at the end of a telephone call. This final summary also indicates you want that call to end.

Here are five difficult situations. Choose the best phrase to deal with the situation appropriately.

Situation	Phrase
1. The speaker is speaking very quickly.	A. I'd like to come in here if I may.
2. The speaker is using very complex, sophisticated language.	B. Sorry what did you mean when you said....?"
3. The speaker uses a word you have never heard before.	C. Could you take it a bit more slowly please?
4. The speaker just keeps on talking.	D. Could you speak more slowly and clearly for me please? – I'm French.
5. The speaker has a strong regional accent.	E. I'm afraid I didn't catch most of that.

The answers are in the footnotes.[15]

Few people have had much training in listening. Living in a competitive culture, most of us are most of the time chiefly concerned with getting our own view across, and we tend to find other people's speeches a tedious interruption of our own ideas.
S.I. Hayakawa, How to Attend a Conference

38. Interact

Communication is most effective when it is a two-way process. Let your English-speaking business partners know that you are actively involved in trying to understand what they are saying. Here are some tips.

a. Listen actively

Active listening helps you concentrate on what another person is saying. You can use body language signals like nodding to show you understand and to encourage the other person to continue. Or you can use words and phrases like *"Right", "I see", and "OK"* for the same purpose. To confirm your understanding, you can repeat key words to check – *"Thursday?" "2 o'clock?", "London?".* You can even repeat a whole sentence or phrase if you want to make absolutely sure – *"So you'll be arriving in London at 2 o'clock."*

b. Get the main message

Listen for the key words in sentences. Usually these are the words speakers emphasise with their voice. You can often understand the main meaning of a speaker just by identifying the key words even though you miss everything in between:

"…coming…….Saturday………11 o'clock"

c. Listen between the lines

Often what is <u>not</u> said is as important as what <u>is</u> said. For example, if you ask a dinner guest, *"Did you like the special regional sausages?"* and they reply, *"The sauce was lovely",* this probably indicates the sausages were not to their taste.

d. Listen with feeling

Try to understand the feelings behind the words of your speaking partner. Show empathy as well as your understanding of what they actually say.

---

[15] Answers 1 – C 2 – E 3 – B 4 – A 5 - D

For example, if someone says, *"I'm not feeling very well today"* don't simply show you've understood by saying, *"Right."* That sounds disinterested or even rude. Instead show empathy. Say something like, *"I'm sorry to hear that. What's wrong? If I were you, I'd go home after the meeting."*

e. Listen with your eyes

In face-to-face communication, be observant and monitor your speaking partners' body language. Gestures and facial expressions often underline the meaning of what they are saying. Also, you can usually get quite a clear idea of how they feel about the subject you are discussing through their non-verbal signals.

Remember
Listen actively
Get the main message
Listen between the lines
Listen with feeling
Listen with your eyes

History repeats itself because no one listens the first time.

39. Control native speakers

Advanced and native speakers of English can easily dominate second language speakers. Their fluency, wide vocabulary and self-confidence in the language give them a natural advantage. They may also use slang and idiomatic expressions, have a strong regional dialect, speak quickly or use special culture-bound humour.

All of this can make them difficult to understand. Usually native speakers are unaware of the effect they are having until you remind them. Often it is enough to simply ask your native speaker counterpart to slow down or to explain what they mean in another way - and to occasionally remind them that you are not a native speaker yourself. Many native speakers find it incredibly difficult to adapt their language to the international arena. They appreciate it when you gently remind them that they are difficult to understand or are talking too much.

But sometimes, native speakers try to misuse the advantage they have. English is then used as a weapon against you rather than as a tool to create mutual understanding.

Here are some "dirty tricks" you can use as a second language speaker if you suspect this is happening. But be careful.

1. Interrupt the native speaker at regular intervals and ask for an explanation of some item of vocabulary. This will slow them down and break up their train of thought. It might then give you the chance to jump in to give your ideas and opinions.

2. After the native speaker has given a long, fluent input ask them to summarise it in two sentences "So that I'm sure I've understood everything". If you do this occasionally it has the effect of making the native speaker talk more briefly and it also makes them uncertain as to whether they are getting their views across clearly enough.

3. Ask them to explain any culture-bound jokes a second time. A good joke cannot be told twice so don't laugh at the explanation. Simply say, "I see" and carry on.

4. Whenever you think your counterpart is showing linguistic insensitivity, speak a few sentences in your own native language and assume that the native speaker has understood what you have just said. Make them feel insecure too.

5. Discuss how the meeting is being run. In other words, discuss process rather than content. Take up the problem of language imbalance and ask the native speaker how they intend to solve it.

Generally, in our international business communication we want a relationship based on trust and mutual respect. It's only when we feel these are lacking that these "dirty tricks" are applicable (or when you are the buyer!).

So, help your native speaker counterparts to learn to be better speakers of international English. Be polite at first to keep the good relationship – but if all else fails don't be afraid to use some "dirty tricks" to protect yourself and your ideas.

Remember
Native speakers are often unaware of dominating conversations
They need to be reminded and controlled
If all else fails, use some dirty tricks

"It was impossible to get a conversation going; everybody was talking too much."

Yogi Berra

40. Practice listening

Use your ears. English is all around you.

You can tune in to English language radio stations like the BBC World Service. You can listen (and watch) the news on CNN. Both the BBC and CNN news channels have business news slots with an international angle.

- You can buy "talking books" (audio tapes or CDs where actors read an abridged version of best-selling books). Included in these are many books on business. Put the "talking book" in the player in your car and listen whilst driving to work. Let the language flow as you drive.
- Record English business material from the TV or radio, or use a "talking book". Choose a four to five-minute section and listen to it intensively. Listen for as many times it takes you to understand every single word of that particular section. Ask a native speaker for help if necessary.
- You can hire original soundtrack DVDs and video tapes. Get a film or series with business connections (e.g. *The Office* a British business comedy or *The Firm* an American thriller). Start watching it with sub-titles and then when you feel you know what is going on – delete the sub-titles.
- Attend business seminars, lectures and courses where the seminar language is English. Some universities have courses run through the medium of English and international training organisations like Management Centre Europe run international business seminars.
- Go to a theatre production in English. Read about the play beforehand so that you know the outline story.
- You can take your listening a step further by intensive listening practice. Record something from the radio or take a talking book. Select a five-minute section and listen to it again and again until you have understood every single word of it.

- Test your listening skills by taking the five-minute recording. Use it for dictation practice. Write out a transcript of the tape and ask a native speaker or someone else with excellent English skills to check the spelling for you.

Try this listening quiz. Are the following statements true or false?

1. You usually hear what you want to hear.
2. Listening is an easy thing to do.
3. You can learn how to listen.
4. You can't pay attention to one subject for a long time.
5. The talker is mainly responsible for the message getting through.
6. Your background, education and culture determine what you hear.
7. The non-verbal signals are not as important as the verbal messages.
8. You listen more carefully to messages about yourself.
9. Listening is more difficult when you are emotional.
10.You shouldn't judge the speaker as they are talking.

Check your answers:

1. True. We interpret messages from our own point of view.
2. False. It requires a great deal of concentration.
3. True. You can learn listening techniques and apply them.
4. True. We need variety and stimulation.
5. False. The responsibility for successful communication lies with both parties.
6. True. These factors colour your perception.
7. False. Both are equally important.
8. True. We relate more easily to topics that are personal.
9. True. Emotions cloud our ability to listen rationally.
10. True. You need to analyse what you are hearing internally. But try not to make judgements too quickly.

How did you get on? The aim of this short test was simply to ask you to think a little about how and why you listen in the way you do. You can change your approach with a bit of practice.

Remember:

Think about how you listen

Define the things you need to improve

Practice, practice, practice

Business vocabulary

"All I know is what I have words for."
Ludwig Wittgenstein

"Words don't come easy to me…" This is the first line of an 80's pop song by FR David. And it seems to sum up the feelings of many learners of English as a second language. When asked what the main problems people have with English, the most common answers are "I need more words", "My vocabulary needs to be wider" or "I have to hesitate to find the right word".

The English language has a rich vocabulary based on a mixture of Latin, French, Germanic and Scandinavian languages with a seasoning of words from Africa, the Middle East and Asia. The Standard Oxford Dictionary has over half a million entries! This is the bad news for people learning English. But there is some good news. Experts estimate that we only need an active vocabulary of about 4000 words to be able to function effectively internationally. With the right 4000 we can make excellent presentations in English, run and take part in meetings, negotiate, write clearly and deal with difficult telephone calls.

Tips 41 – 45 will help you take some steps on the way to build that 4000-word vocabulary.

41. Activate your words

There are three questions we need to answer. How many words do I have at the moment? How do I identify the extra words I need? How do I then learn the words identified?

It is very difficult to measure accurately a person's active vocabulary – that is the words you can actually use. Linguists often use a ratio of three passive words to one active word as a rough guide. Some studies have been made with business people in Germany and Sweden. Those with a higher education background who use their English regularly but have not lived in an English-speaking country have active vocabularies of between 2500 and 3500 words.

There are several ways of identifying the words you need. Most of the reading we do in English for our work is extensive reading. In other words, we don't try to understand every single word but try to get the overall message and understand the main ideas. Just occasionally read a fax, part of a report or magazine article intensively i.e. making sure you understand every word and idea. Pull out and write down the words or phrases that you judge to be useful so that you can learn them later. Do the same when listening to your native-speaker colleagues in meetings or on the phone. Pick up just one word per meeting and write it down. Then use your dictionary as an identification tool. Whenever you look up a word in the dictionary, make a pencil mark next to it. If you look that word up a second time you need to know it – pull it out and write it down. In this way you can build up your own vocabulary list of words to be learnt. Once you have identified these relevant words or phrases you then need to learn them.

Everyone learns in different ways but here are some tips that work with most people: -

1) Use post-its

Take a word you want to learn. Write it on a post-it with the translation on the back. Stick it on your PC screen or phone. Every time you use the PC or pick up the phone, test yourself. You soon fix that word in your memory.

2) Use native-speakers

Use the coffee breaks in meetings to ask native speakers to explain unfamiliar words they used in the meeting itself. Many native-speakers love the unofficial teacher role so make the most of it. (You can also do this during the meeting but generally it's better to discuss the linguistic aspects as part of small talk.)

3) Use a notebook

Draw four columns on the page. In the first column write the new word. In the second column the phrase or sentence in which you found it. The third column has an explanation or synonym from your English-English dictionary and the last column the translation. This process helps in learning not only the meaning but also the usage of your new word.

4) Talk to yourself.

Although this is considered the first sign of madness it's also a very good way to practice vocabulary. For example, simply sit on your chair in your office and describe what you see on your desk, on the walls and outside the window. Think of a business process you are familiar with and describe it in English e.g. *How to fill in an insurance claim form* or *The best way to use a particular software package* or *Our main product's manufacturing process.*

5) Use your left hand.
If you want to remember a key word or a word you always forget, write it three times with your left hand (or right hand if you are left-handed). This helps fix the word in your memory.

6) Count words
When you learn a new word see how many times you can read it or hear it over the next month. Write down the context in which it was used.
7) Find a partner
Find an email partner. Each day send your partner a new word that you have found. The partner then sends it back used in a sentence. If you don't have an email partner log on to www.owad.de and you will be sent one word every day for free.

Remember:
Test your word power
Identify the words you need
Learn in different ways

> *"One forgets words as one forgets names. One's vocabulary needs constant fertilizing, or it will die."*
>
> *Evelyn Waugh*

42. Be creative
You're in the middle of a sentence. Suddenly the word you knew two minutes ago has disappeared from your brain. Your English-speaking guest looks at you questioningly as you hesitate - but all you can think of is the word in your own language. Your mind goes blank.

All of us have been in that situation at one time or another. We feel stressed and irritated with ourselves as we fail to get our message across clearly. So, what can we do about it? How can we overcome those memory lapses?

We need to be creative in our approach to vocabulary. This means using the words we know in as creative and flexible a way as possible. And to do this we need to steal some of the trade secrets of English teachers. When you think about it, English teachers use a wide variety of methods to explain words to students. We can use some of these secrets to find alternative ways of explaining the words we've forgotten or even to explain concepts where we don't actually know the correct English word.

Let's look at some examples. Let's imagine you are in the middle of a conversation with an English-speaking business partner and you get stuck on the word *"Purchaser"*. Let's see how many ways there might be of getting the concept across to the other person.

- You can try to find a word that means the same – *"Buyer"*.
  The English language is rich in synonyms or near synonyms.
- Find the opposite – *"Seller"*
  It's often easy to explain what the word doesn't mean and get the meaning over in that way.
- Look for an example – *"Mr Matthews has this position in your company."*
  If your business partner knows Mr Matthews and what he does, this is probably the easiest way of explaining what you mean.
- Describe the word you are looking for – *"It's the person who buys things for your company. It could be raw materials, office equipment or spare parts for example."*
  This usually takes longer but is easy for the speaker.
- Put the word into a sentence – *"If I want to sell something to a company, I try to make an appointment with the Purchaser."*
  This puts the word in a context that is self-explanatory.
- Find words associated with the concept – *Offer, bid, pay for, payment, consignee, customer, acquire....*

Here you're playing a word association game, which can be fun
– rather like playing a party game.
- Just say the word for "*Purchaser*" in your own language.
  Many people understand more than they can speak
  and are often familiar with words in their line of business.
- Use your hands
  For certain concepts you can use gestures to describe them.
  For example, it's easier to describe a spiral staircase using
  your hand in a corkscrew motion rather than trying to find
  the appropriate words and geometric terms.
- Draw a picture
  This is very useful when explaining technical details or when
  your business partner has very limited English language skill.

If one of the above techniques fails, then jump straight to an alternative. If
you practice this, you will find that those embarrassing moments get less
and less frequent and that you gain more and more confidence. And the
more confident you are, the less stress you feel. Then those words you
knew two minutes ago are less likely to disappear in the first place.

Imagine you are talking to an English-speaking business associate. Try to
explain the following four words using the techniques we suggest.

1. *Shares*   Find a synonym and make a description.
2. *Credit card*   Find an example and put the word in a sentence.
3. *Chairman*   Find associated words and make a description.
4. *Wealthy*   Find a synonym and the opposite.

You can find the answers in the footnotes.[16]

---

[16] 1. Stocks. You own these when you invest in a company.   2. Mastercard. You can use a **credit card** to buy goods instead of using money.   3. Meeting, leader, facilitator, agenda, minutes. This person is a man in charge of running a meeting.   4. Rich. Poor.

Remember
Be creative
Be flexible in your approach
Use your English teacher's trade secrets

> *Creative thinking is not a talent. It can be learnt.*
> *Edward de Bono*

43. Avoid being egocentric

When Mrs Thatcher was the British Prime Minister, a reporter asked her how she felt now that her son had a baby. "Oh, it's marvellous!" she supposedly replied, "We have finally become a grandmother!" The next day in one of the tabloid papers there was a picture of Mrs Thatcher with a crown on her head and the headline – "Maggie for Queen".

Mrs Thatcher had accidentally used the royal *"we"* to describe herself in the same way that the British royal family traditionally does. The immediate reaction of the press and public was that she was no longer satisfied with being just the Prime Minister but now wanted to become the Queen as well!

We can all laugh at the stereotype of the power-hungry politician but sometimes we can sound the same ourselves.

You frequently hear presentations like this:

"I am very happy to be here and I want to tell you about our new projects. We in the Sales Department want the rest of the company to understand what we are doing. I think it is necessary for us to inform the rest of you in detail so that we know you are working to support us properly.

I would like to start by outlining the two product launches we plan for next month, then I will outline what we expect from you and finally I want to show the new logo we have introduced into the international market."

If I were in the audience I would feel totally alienated by the speaker's style. Everything is presented from the speaker's point of view or from the point of view of the Sales Department. If we want to influence others our language needs to reflect a co-operative and empathetic attitude. We need to put ourselves in the shoes of the people we are speaking or writing to.

We need to see the world from their perspective and address their concerns.

The word "*I*" is a distancing word that separate us from the very people we want to connect with. And usually we do it accidentally. We use phrases such as "*I think*", "*I hope*", "*I want to...*", "*I would like to...*" without thinking of the impact they might have on the audience or reader. What we need to do is use the words "*you*", "*us*" and the inclusive "*we*" which means both the speaker and the listeners.

How would this affect the short, egocentric presentation we looked at?

Thank you for inviting me to present and discuss together the Sales Department's new projects. It's important for us all to understand what's happening in the company so that we can support each other in the best way.

Firstly, let us look at the two product launches planned for next month, then discuss how we can co-operate on these to get the best result and finally let's get your reactions on the new logo for the international market."

Sometimes you need to show your personal beliefs or strength of opinion and then the word "*I*" really means something. But don't dilute this powerful effect by overusing egocentric language. As a rough rule of thumb, for every "*I*" you use in a presentation or email, you need to use "*you*", the inclusive "*we*" or "*us*" five times to counteract that egocentric effect.

> *"Self-interest is the enemy of all true affection."*
> Franklin D Roosevelt

44. Always look on the bright side of life

"Always Look On The Bright Side Of Life" was an unexpected hit song taken from Monty Python's film "Life of Brian". It appealed to young and old alike. The song said that because you know things will always go wrong you might as well enjoy whatever you can. As someone else once said, "Both optimists and pessimists succeed or fail to the same degree – it's just that optimists have more fun on the way!"

But if you listen to the way we use our English at work you'd think that most of us are out and out pessimists. We love to look on the dark side of life and to pass on our gloom to everyone we talk to. Have a look at the first example.

1. *I'm afraid you can't call back after five as our office is closed then*
Now, do I really want to know when I can't call or when the office is closed? No, of course not. I want to know when your office is open and when I <u>can</u> call. It would create a much more positive feeling to say: *You are welcome to call our office any time between 9 and 5.*

Here are five more examples. Look at the negative sentence and the explanation. Then try to make a positive sentence yourself. You will find the answers in the footnotes.[17]

2. *I'm sorry but John will be ten minutes late so the meeting will be delayed.*
Now we'll all be blaming John and feeling irritated. But ten minutes isn't so bad. With the right atmosphere it will seem like no time at all.

3. *I won't be back before two tomorrow afternoon.*
But when will you be back? Think positive! Make me feel you want me to contact you.

4. *I'm sorry I don't speak French.*
That's probably true if you answer a French speaker in English! Help them. Offer alternatives.

5. *I don't know. Maybe someone else can help you.*
This sounds negative and not at all confident. Be more definite and be clearer about possible help.

6. *Don't hesitate to call if you have any problems.*
I really dislike this phrase. You hear it everywhere, but that doesn't mean to say it's a good expression to use. Why should I hesitate? Simply mentioning it makes me think I ought to hesitate! Also, the word "any" often indicates that you expect a negative response. And finally, why should I

---

[17] 2. John will be with us in ten minutes. Would you like another cup of coffee? 3. I'll be back after two tomorrow afternoon. 4. Sorry, but could we take this in English or German? 5. Let me put you in touch with someone in our Finance Department. I'm sure they will be able to help you. 6. Please call if you have some questions.

have "problems"? This word is over-used by second language speakers of English. Look for a more positive approach.

Ask yourself if you regularly use negative words like: problem, impossible, can't, don't, bad, awful, delay, late, not available. Replace them with less depressing expressions and try to think positively.
Also think about the way you say things. Some second language speakers are a little afraid to put too much stress or emphasis on words in case they get it wrong. But if your intonation is flat and monotonous it sounds as if you are bored with everyone and everything.

Remember
A bit of energy in the voice, a positive choice of vocabulary and a smile makes all the difference - helping you and those you meet to always look on the bright side of life.

> *Whenever I hear somebody sigh, "Life is hard." I am tempted*
> *to ask," Compared to what?"*
>
> *Sydney Harris*

45. Avoid false friends

"With friends like you, who needs enemies!" We say this when our friends let us down or work against our interests. When we are using a second language, we need to avoid the vocabulary that lets us down or works against our interests!
English has a great many words in common with other languages. Let's use German as an example. It's estimated that there are about 30 000 words which are more or less the same or similar between English and German. At the simplest level you have words like "hand", "finger" and "arm". Or words that are easily recognisable like "comical", "clinic" and "author". In certain professional fields a great many English words have been assimilated into German. This is certainly true of high-tech areas and is often due to the influence of the United States. You see words like "marketing", "consortium", "network" and "computer" in the German press every day.

Moreover, there are some words that have travelled in the opposite direction – from German to English. Here are three examples from different fields – "angst", "blitz" and "rucksack".

And what's true for German is true for many other languages too –but to different degrees. Many of the formal words in English are Latin or French based and are easily recognised and learnt by romance language speakers. These words in common can be described as "Instant English" for second language speakers. And that's good news for learners of English. But there's some bad news too! There are two or three hundred words which look as if they are "Instant English" but aren't. These we call "False Friends". And they are often a reason for misunderstandings in international business meetings.

Here's a short presentation made by a native German speaker in English. It includes 10 key German "False Friends". See if you can identify them, then check with the correct version below.

"My chief asked me to give you our prospects. If you control the backside, you can see the actual price list. We undertakers shouldn't be too sensible, but we can eventually discuss adjusting prices to our competition. My meaning is that we must not do it yet."

What the speaker should have said is:

"My head of department (boss) asked me to give you our brochures. If you check the back page you can see the current price list. We entrepreneurs shouldn't be too sensitive, but we can possibly discuss adjusting prices to our competition. My opinion is that we don't have to do it yet."

Often, we know intellectually which words are "False Friends" and which aren't. The problem is that in the heat of the discussion the word from our own language pops into our mind. We translate it directly and, if it's a "False Friend", incorrectly. Our colleagues who also speak the same language don't help, because they understand the "False Friend" perfectly!

We have to become "False Friend" detectives.

- Look for clues in the facial expression of your native-speaker business colleagues. When you see a look of slight puzzlement or when the eyes glaze over for a second – stop and check you are both talking about the same thing.
- Look up "False Friends" on the internet. You will find a variety of sites specialising in "False Friends" for your mother tongue.
- Make a "False Friend" mini-dictionary based on your experience and reading. There are usually twenty to thirty key "False Friends" for speakers of European languages. These are the words that radically change the listeners understanding of what is being said.

Here's an example from German:

1. aktuell	current/latest	(not "actual")
2. baksida	back/reverse	(not "backside")
3. bekommen	get	(not "become")
4. chef	boss/manager/head of…	(not "chief")
5. eventuell	perhaps/possibly	(not "eventually")
6. gultig	valid	(not "guilty")
7. konsequent	consistent	(not "consequent")
8. kontrollieren	check/inspect	(not "control")
9. mappe	folder/file	(not "map")
10. meinung	opinion	(not "meaning")
11. muss nicht	don't have to	(not "must not")
12. personal	personnel/staff	(not "personal")
13. prospekte	brochure	(not "prospect")
14. provision	commission	(not "provision")
15. prufen	check/test	(not "prove")
16. rabatt	discount	(not "rebate")
17. rezept	prescription	(not "recipe")
18. sensibel	sensitive	(not "sensible")
19. sympathisch	nice/pleasant	(not "sympathetic")
20. warenhaus	department store	(not "warehouse")

Remember
"Instant English" increases your word power
Become a "False Friend" detective
Avoid the 20 to 30 worst ones

English is such a deliciously complex and undisciplined language, we can bend, fuse, distort words to all our purposes. We give old words new meanings, and we borrow new words from any language that intrudes into our intellectual environment.

Willard Gaylin

Grammar

"Even kings must obey the laws of grammar."
Moliere

Many of us hated grammar lessons at school. We sometimes wondered what the relevance was to actually speaking the language. But we also recognised that a language needs a structure and rules on which we can hang the vocabulary. It's just that we often feel insecure and unsure about whether we are using those rules correctly. Imagine you have been asked to assess how correctly you use English grammar on a scale from zero to 100. Zero means you make a mistake in every sentence you say. 100 means you never make a mistake. Many second language speakers will place themselves at 50% - in other words they feel they make mistakes in every other sentence. If you put yourself at this level or feel unsure about your grammar, tips 46 – 50 will help you improve those percentages.

46. Assess your grammar
There is some bad news about grammar and some good news! Let's take the bad news first. Like every major world language English has a complicated grammar system. For example, there are supposedly over three hundred forms of the conditional sentence in English – *"If you were of the opinion that English grammar was easy then maybe it might have been better for you to skip this module."* There are grammar books several hundred pages long explaining the intricacies of the different systems. Second language students struggle to make sense of complicated grammar lessons and wonder if it helps them to really communicate better.
But there is also some good news. If you analyse the use of verb systems in English you will find that, in speech, native speakers only use four key systems eighty per cent of the time. This means that if we can get these four systems right – we can be at least eighty per cent correct when speaking! So, let's assess your competence in these four systems. The next module then shows how the systems should be used.

Here are twelve sentences. Put the verb in the correct form in the sentence.

1. I ------- that watch for my birthday last year. *(get)*
2. The Heads of Department ------- every Monday. *(meet)*
3. I ------- with friends at the moment. *(stay)*
4. I ------- here for five years. *(work)*
5. They ------- in Sweden ten years ago. *(live)*
6. Water ------- at 100 degrees Centigrade. *(boil)*
7. Don't disturb him now, he -------. *(sleep)*
8. John ------- as an accountant since 2001. *(work)*
9. David ------- Lisa yesterday evening. *(see)*
10. On Fridays Frank normally ------- home a little earlier. *(go)*
11. Hurry up, we ------- for you! *(wait)*
12. We ------- each other every day for the last two years. *(phone)*

Let's see how you got on.
We've tested the four main grammar systems in the following way:
Sentences 1, 5 and 9 test the first system – the Simple Past.
Sentences 2, 6 and 10 test the second system – the Simple Present.
Sentences 3, 7 and 11 test the third system – the Present Continuous.
Sentences 4, 8 and 12 test the fourth system – the Present Perfect.
So, let's go through them in that order.

The Simple Past - 1. *got*   5. *lived*   9. *Saw*

The Simple Present - 2. *meet* 6. *boils* 10. *Goes*

The Present Continuous - 3. *am staying* 7. *is sleeping* 11. *are waiting*

The Present Perfect - 4. *have worked (or have been working)*   8. *has worked (or has been working)* 12. *have phoned (or have been phoning)*

How did you get on? If you had no problems with this short test then you can skip the next section. But if you made some mistakes go through the next tip – Know your basics.

These four systems are the foundations of your English grammar. In an ideal world you should not be making any mistakes with them at all. Certainly, the more able you are to use these systems correctly the clearer your messages become. You would then have a stable platform on which to build both your spoken and your written English.

Remember
In 80% of your spoken English you only need to use four grammar systems.

> *"When money talks nobody notices what grammar it uses."*
> *Anonymous*

47. Know your basics
Now let's have a look at how you should use the four systems correctly. Remember that in the English language there are always exceptions to every rule! So, this is a rough and ready (but effective) guide to basic English grammar.

- System 1 – the Simple Past.
  This grammar system is used to describe actions that are over, done or completed. In other words, they are not going on now. For example, you would use the Simple Past in answer to the question "Did…?"
  When did you live in Oxford?
  I lived in Oxford twenty years ago.
  This tells the questioner quite clearly that you no longer live in Oxford.
  Certain time words indicate the use of the Simple Past e.g. *ago, before, yesterday, last year/month/week.*
  The verb in the Simple Past usually has an *–ed* ending except for the infamous irregular verbs that our teachers loved to test! But because they loved to test us on these, we are generally quite good at them. The other piece of good news is that even if we get it wrong and make our irregular verbs regular – it's perfectly under-

standable. The only problem is that it sounds a bit childish to native speakers whose children might well say, *"Daddy, I <u>runned</u> all the way home today."*

- System 2 – the Simple Present
This grammar system is used to describe actions that are a permanent part of your everyday life. It does not tell us what is happening just at this moment but is a more general description. For example, you would use this system to answer the question "Do / Does…?"
Where do you live?
I live in London
From this it is clear that London is your permanent home and that you do not intend to move soon.
Where does she live?
She live<u>s</u> in London
Don't forget the "S" on the end when you are talking in the third person.
Often you will find certain adverbs in Simple Present sentences. These adverbs describe how often the action takes place e.g. *always, usually, frequently, sometimes occasionally, seldom, never.*
I never smoke cigars. I sometimes go for a run. I always have a glass of wine on a Friday evening.

- System 3 – the Present Continuous
We use this system to describe the world around us – what's happening just now.
You would use the Present Continuous to answer the question "Are / Is….?"
Where are you staying this week?
I'm staying with a friend in France.
The feeling here is that you are telling us what's happening right at the moment but that it is also temporary. It will change soon like the weather – *It's raining at the moment.* But it will soon stop!
Time phrases used with this system mean "now" e.g. *at the moment, at present, right now, just now* or as some politicians love to say, *at this particular moment in history.*

- System 4 – the Present Perfect

  The Present Perfect acts as a bridge between the past and the present. It describes an action that started in the past and which is still going on (or has just finished).

  You would use this system to answer the question "Has / have….?)

  How long have you lived in London?

  I have lived there for ten years.

  (An alternative form of this system is "been living" – *How long have you been living in London?*)

  You are still living in London although it might be you might be on the point of leaving or have just left. We will have to wait for you to give us further information before we know if that is the case.

  There are two key time words we use with the Present Perfect – *for* and *since.*

  For tells us how long the action has taken – *for ten years.*

  Since tells us when the action started – *since 1997*

When we speak the two most important grammar systems are the Simple Past and the Simple Present. According to some linguists we use these systems for over 60% of our spoken English.

Don't mix up the Present Continuous with the Present Simple. If you say, *"I'm working for Taylor and Sons."* It gives the feeling that you are a temporary member of staff or that you intend to leave the company soon. It can undermine your professional credibility. *"I work for Taylor and Sons."* Shows you are a permanent member of staff and that you intend to remain one.

Remember:

The Simple Past is used to describe actions that are over, done or completed.

The Simple Present is used to describe actions that are a permanent part of your everyday life.

The Present Continuous describes the world around us – what's happening just now.

The Present Perfect acts as a bridge between the past and the present.

For everything there is a season,
And a time for every matter under heaven:
A time to be born, and a time to die;
A time to plant, and a time to pluck up what is planted;
A time to kill, and a time to heal;
A time to break down, and a time to build up;
A time to weep, and a time to laugh;
A time to mourn, and a time to dance;
A time to throw away stones, and a time to gather stones together;
A time to embrace, And a time to refrain from embracing;
A time to seek, and a time to lose;
A time to keep, and a time to throw away;
A time to tear, and a time to sew;
A time to keep silence, and a time to speak;
A time to love, and a time to hate,
A time for war, and a time for peace.

> *Ecclesiastes 3:1-8*

48. Look to the future

Albert Einstein once said, "I never think of the future, it comes soon enough." But, in fact, we spend a lot of time planning for the future both in our work and in our social lives. We have to remember that the future can be seen and described in different ways depending on our circumstances. And we need to make these different circumstances clear to our international business partners.

Most second language speakers of English mainly use the verb "will" to talk about the future. Surprisingly, this is not the most common future form when native speakers talk together.

There are four main future verb forms in English and each form has a slightly different meaning: -

1) The Simple Present

This is used in the very specific situation of describing an itinerary e.g.

"On Monday I fly to New York and on Tuesday meet Howard Green. Then on Wednesday I travel to Washington and visit our office there. On Friday morning I see Mike and then fly back Friday evening."

The feeling here is that everything has been decided and is in place. The tickets are booked and the arrangements made.

2) The "-ing" form

This is also used for actions that have already been decided and which will take place in the very near future. But the actions don't have to be in the form of an itinerary e.g.

"Tonight, we're having dinner with friends. We're meeting at Harry's bar."

"The Chairman is speaking to all the staff tomorrow because we are opening new offices in London and Berlin."

3) "will"

"Will" is used in two different future scenarios: -

a) For predicting what you think could happen e.g.

"I think the rate of unemployment will decrease over the next six months."

"British car-makers will be faced with problems because of exchange rates."

b) For promises, offers and threats e.g.

"I will make sure you get the information by Monday."

"I'll get you a cup of tea."

"We won't sign the contract today."

Remember "won't" is the short form of "will not".

Do remember also that the use of "shall" has changed from the time many of us were at school. We were told to use "shall" in the first person e.g. *"I shall see him next week."* In fact, we only use "shall" in two situations nowadays. Firstly, in legal documents – *"The two parties shall agree to the following terms."* And secondly when making an offer in the form of a question – *"Shall I open the window?"*

4) "going to"

This is the most common way to talk about the future and the most flexible. It is used for plans and intentions e.g.

"He's going to move to Spain when he retires."

"I'm going to visit my parents at the weekend."

"The company is going to install a new production line when there's more cash available."

The feeling here is not of 100% certainty and that's why native speakers use it so much. It allows for a change of mind or a change in the circumstances. So be a little careful if a native speaker uses this form rather than "will" when making a promise!

These four future forms overlap in usage. And the rules are not exact. Native speakers use the forms instinctively and sometimes incorrectly. But if you do get mixed up, just remember the English saying, "Don't worry, it may never happen!"

Remember:

The Simple Present - This is used in the very specific situation of describing an itinerary.

The "-ing" form - This is used for actions that have already been decided and which will take place in the very near future.

"Will" – Used a) For predicting what you think could happen b) For promises, offers and threats

"going to" - This is the most common way to talk about the future and the most flexible. It is used for plans and intentions

> *"The best thing about the future is that it only comes one day at a time."*
> *Abraham Lincoln*

49. Get your timing right

"What exactly is the delivery date for the goods?" "How long is the contract valid?" "When will the meeting be held?" "At what time will you be back in the office?"

We all have to be able to answer these questions from our international business partners accurately and clearly. And to do this we need to be able to use the correct prepositions of time.

Most learners of English as a second language groan and sigh when the word "preposition" is mentioned. We've been told that there aren't any rules and that it's a question of language sensitivity or luck as to whether you choose the right preposition in the right place. This may be true for some areas where we need to use prepositions but it is certainly not true for prepositions of time. And there is some other good news too. For much of the time we only need three key time prepositions!

Let's first of all look at these three key prepositions and see how they should be used. Then we'll look at four other prepositions that make up a large part of the remainder.

Here are the big three: **In – On – At**

With these prepositions you can deal with most of your time arrangements.

in – for years, months and seasons

In 2003   In August   In the winter

on – for days, days + part of the day, dates and special days

On Monday   On Thursday afternoon   On 22 September   On Good Friday

at – for times, mealtimes, festivals, the weekend and night

At 3 o'clock   At lunchtime   At Christmas   At the weekend   At night

Now let's look at the other four: **By – For – Since – From…to…**

With these prepositions you can deal with most of the other situations.

by – this means "at the latest"

I should be back by 2 o'clock   We must meet by May 10 at the latest

for – shows how long an action has lasted - a period of time.

He has lived in Berlin for ten years   He worked in Africa for six months

since – describes a point in time when an action started in the past – an action which is still going on.

I have worked in London since 1995   I have been waiting here since two o'clock

from…to… – the starting and closing points of an action.

Our office is open from 9 to 5   I lived in London from 1996 to 1999

Armed with these prepositions you can happily make your business arrangements without the fear of turning up on the wrong day at the wrong time!

Finally, test yourself. Put the correct preposition in each sentence.

1) My birthday is __ April.

2) We eat eggs__ Easter.

3) Call me __ two o'clock at the latest.

4) He was free __ May to September.

5) Let's meet __ June 3.

6) She lived there __ ten years.

7) He has waited __ 9 o'clock.

Here are the answers:
1) in 2) at 3) by 4) from 5) on 6) for 7) since)

Remember
in – for years, months and seasons
on – for days, days + part of the day, dates and special days
at – for times, mealtimes, festivals, the weekend and night

> *"They say that time changes things, but you have to actually change them yourself."*
>
> Andy Warhol

50. Keep improving

With the help of a few simple exercises you can practice and improve your grammar in English.

1. Copy an article from a trade magazine. Read it through and then use Tippex to blank out all the prepositions. The next day try to fill in the blanks.
2. Copy another article and do the same – but this time Tippex out ten verbs. This also practices vocabulary. You need to find a verb that fits the sentence and then put it into the correct form.
3. Ask a friend to type out ten sentences from your magazine in large typeface. Your friend then cuts up each sentence into individual words and puts each sentence in an envelope. Your task is to reconstruct the sentences so that they make sense and then decide on which order the sentences came in the article. This practices word order and general comprehension.
4. Teach your children the four main tenses in English (The Present Simple, the Present Continuous, The Simple Past and the Past Perfect) and how they are used. If you cannot do this, you need to reread tip 46!
5. Talk to yourself again. Describe your week. Tell yourself what you have done and when, what you are doing and what you are going to do in the future. Try to be accurate. Note when you feel unsure about what you are saying and check with tip 47.

Don't get depressed if you still feel unsure. Trust your intuition. What you learnt at school is often still there in the back of your mind. And even if you get the grammar wrong it's not the end of the world. Usually you are still understood and often you can correct yourself later in the conversation. When you are writing, your grammar checker will help you enormously even though it too can make mistakes. Correct grammar helps get your messages across more clearly. But remember that it is only part of a whole arsenal of the language skills you have to make yourself understood.

Remember:
Practice helps
Trust yourself
Grammar is only part of correct communication

Conclusions

"Self-confidence is not a feeling of superiority, but of independence."

Lama Yeshe

We all make mistakes

We all make mistakes. But when we make them in a second language it somehow seems worse. It's as if our old school teacher is looking over our shoulder with a red pen ready to run it through the wrong choice of vocabulary or the wrong grammatical construction. At school we were graded according to the number of mistakes we made in a test and the demand was for perfection – 10 out of 10. But out of the classroom language is not a perfect communication tool. It is subject to changing linguistic fashions, personal styles and cultural differences. Language is a living, imperfect method for exchanging messages.

So, how important is it to avoid making mistakes when using English as a second language speaker?

There are three main categories of mistake – rather like the colours of a set of traffic lights.

The "red light" mistakes are those mistakes that change the meaning of what you are saying or make the message totally incomprehensible. For example, there is the misuse of "false friend" vocabulary. If you say, *"I will eventually meet you at the pub this evening."* – and you really mean, *"I will possibly meet you at the pub this evening."* – this could create a definite misunderstanding and irritation! Or you might mispronounce words so as to change their meaning – *"My husband is a eunuch and impotent man"* rather than *"a unique and important man"*! Usually such "red light" mistakes are in these false friend or pronunciation categories and knowing this can motivate you to speak clearly and learn to avoid the twenty worst false friends.

The "amber light" mistakes are to do with poor intonation and stress and wrong level of formality. The meaning of the words is clear, but the feeling is wrong. For example, if you put the stress on the wrong word in the sentence, you change the emphasis – *"I **know** how you feel"* means you've told me many times whereas *"I know how **you** feel"* means I haven't had the chance to let you know my feelings.

Many of us use over formal language when it isn't appropriate because that's how we were taught in school years ago. A very simple example is the use of the word *"persons"*. In ordinary speech the plural of *"person"* is *"people"*. But many German speakers, for example, say things like, *"There were six persons at the meeting."* This accidently makes the meeting sound very formal as we only use the plural form *"persons"* in legal documents these days. It's the same with the word *"shall"* which many second language speakers use with the first person when talking about the future – *"I shall send you the draft next week."* Native speakers now use *"will"* in this situation or avoid the problem by using the short form – *"I'll send you the draft next week."* We now mainly use *"shall"* in legal English or when making a polite offer in the form of a question – *"Shall I open the window?"*

"Green light" mistakes are all those small cosmetic errors, which do not prevent the meaning from being understood. This could be, for example, leaving the *"s"* off the verb – *"She drive to work every day"* - or using the wrong preposition – *"I will meet him at Wednesday"* rather than *"on Wednesday"*. The meaning is still clear, but it just sounds a little clumsy. "Green light" mistakes are not a problem except if you make a lot of them and people start to listen for the mistake rather than the content of what you are saying.

So, mistakes matter – but not as much as we tend to think. Mistakes can be corrected and misunderstandings can be overcome. The danger is when our demand for perfection makes us think too much before saying something. In a meeting we want to contribute but often try to work out the perfect sentence in our heads before opening our mouths. And when we finally do speak – they've changed the subject and our perfect English sentence is now perfectly useless!

> *"The only real mistake is the one from which we learn nothing."*
> John Powell

The future starts here

If you are serious about starting to improve your business English (and you probably are if you've read this far!) – then start practicing today.

Make a simple study guide for yourself based on your self-assessment. Start by choosing exercises and ideas you will enjoy or find easy to do – or both. In other words, look for small wins – thing you can do quickly and easily.

- Decide on three small wins that you can start doing today.
- Specify a clear goal for each win.
- Give a realistic time frame.
- Reward yourself for each win you complete.

Remember the saying, "When all is said and done there is usually more said than done." So, take a leaf out of the Nike advert and "Just Do It!" Do it today.

www.ingramcontent.com/pod-product-compliance
Lightning Source LLC
Chambersburg PA
CBHW070043210526
45170CB00012B/575